How to Achieve

YOUniversal Prosperity™

And Experience Health, Happiness,
Inner Peace, and Financial Freedom …
In Less Time Than You Might Think

Rev. Dr. Bil Holton

Rev. Dr. Cher Holton

Prosperity Publishing House

Copyright ©2021 Bil Holton, Cher Holton
All rights reserved.

Reproduction or translation of any part of this work beyond that permitted by Section 107 or 108 of the 1976 United States Copyright Act without the permission of the copyright owner is unlawful. Requests for permission or further information should be addressed to the authors, c/o Prosperity Publishing House, 1405 Autumn Ridge Drive, Durham, NC 27712.

This publication is designed to provide accurate and authoritative information in regard to the subject matter covered. It is sold with the understanding that the publisher is not engaged in rendering legal, accounting, or other professional service. If legal advice or other expert assistance is required, the services of a competent professional person should be sought. *From a Declaration of Principles jointly adopted by a Committee of the American Bar Association and a Committee of Publishers.*

Prosperity Publishing House
   Durham, NC

Library of Congress Cataloging-in-Publication Data

Holton, Bil and Cher Holton
How to Achieve YOUniversal Prosperity / Bil Holton and Cher Holton
p. cm.

      ISBN 978-1-946291-11-0
      1. Spiritual   2. New Thought   3. Self Help
      4. Financial
      II. Title

Library of Congress Control Number: 2021930072
Printed in the United States of America

10 9 8 7 6 5 4 3 2 1

Dedication

We're dedicating this book of Y☯Universal Prosperity™ teachings to those people who are on a higher consciousness path toward their spiritual growth, with the following insights that represent all of our journeys through a sometimes chaotic, other times joyful, earth experience, which we call skin school:

The key to Y☯Universal Prosperity™ and mastering the art of living in a chaotic world lies in understanding the working principles that align your human self with your Higher Self. The capital 'S' Self is your Super Self, your Divine Nature, what we call the Extraordinary You.

This book is dedicated to those who understand that we are all the individualized Life Force, the Image of our GOD Essence (our Global Omnipresent Divine Nature) actualizing through our Divine Nature as us in human form. This individualized Life Force is our Soul Signature and timeless Personal Identity in the Cosmos. So, in whatever dimension of being we find ourselves, we'll be recognized and others will be recognized, because they too, will have their own distinctive Soul Signature.

Contents

Introduction 1

Part 1: Y☯Universal Prosperity's 7 Principles 11

Part 2: The 4 Core Benefits of Achieving Y☯Universal Prosperity
 – and How to Maximize Them 47
    How to Use the Y☯Universal Prosperity Tips in
        This Section 49
            Health Matters 51
            Happiness Matters 91
            Inner Peace Matters 121
            Financial Freedom Matters 155

Part 3: Understanding Our Human, and Divine Natures Which
    Underwrite Our Prosperity 201
        Our Human Nature Explored 205
        Our Divine Nature Explored 215
        The Powe of OM 220

Part 4: Our Seven Core Abilities 223
        Authentegrity 227
        Intuitive Wisdom 233
        Inner Strength 241
        Optimistic Spirit 249
        Questioning Unquestioned Answers 255
        Self-Reliance 263
        Giving Consciousness 269

The Four Foundational Activities to Include in
    Your Spiritual Practice 275

About the Authors 277
An Invitation From Bil and Cher 278
Other Books by the Holtons 279
Credits and Image Citations 288

Introduction

*H*ave you ever experienced the frustration of hearing about amazing Prosperity Principles, then not being able to manifest them in your own life? Let's begin with a true confession: we studied a lot of traditional courses focused on Prosperity, including some well-known leaders in the New Thought movement. We bought into these teachings and really embraced them. We wrote great denials and powerful affirmations; we visualized vividly, with emotions, color, all the senses involved; we created amazing vision boards, even coming up with our own "brand" that we called "Dreamscapes." We tithed religiously, giving of our time, talents, and treasures. We even fell into the "This or something better" justification when things did not manifest as expected. And we taught these strategies to others in our Prosperity Truth talks and classes.

One day we looked at each other and realized the Principles we were teaching and practicing no longer made sense to us. They did not seem to actually work by any kind of sustainable measure, nor were they replicable in various circumstances. We realized we were being lulled into a host of activities to distract us from the reality that these tools just weren't valid!

Of course, that felt like blasphemy! However, we made a decision ... a powerful decision. We stopped teaching Prosperity – totally! We began what turned out to be a 5-year deep dive into what prosperous people (who are also spiritually enriched and happy) actually do. What separates the way they think and act from the rest of us? Are there any universal Principles that apply, leading to an overall feeling of prosperity and spiritual enrichment? We decided not to teach Prosperity again until we felt we had a real understanding, at a deep level, of what it means to be prosperous. The outcome of this deep dive culminated with this book!

Our prosperity message is based on researching the sixth sense foresight and common sense hindsight of people all over the world who have achieved an overall life experience of prosperity. And while their views of prosperity may differ, they all have four things in common. They agree that when it comes to true prosperity, **health** matters, **happiness** matters, **inner peace** matters, and **financial freedom** matters. We call that marriage between material comforts and spiritual growth Y☯Universal Prosperity.

Discovering how Y☯Universally prosperous you can be is what this life-changing book is all about. Let's get started with our definition of Y☯Universal Prosperity:

> *Getting your Human Nature in sync with your Divine Nature so you can achieve Health, Happiness, Inner Peace, and Financial Freedom in less time than you might think, as you master the art of living in skin school by walking the spiritual path on practical, positive, prosperous feet.*

Let's Talk About Money

Health, Happiness, and Inner Peace can get checked off on just about everyone's list of desired elements for feeling fulfilled – no argument at all. And then there's the issue of money! As soon as the concept of money enters the conversation, strange things start to happen. People want to hem and haw, talking about money not being important while in the same breath affirming a winning lottery ticket for several million dollars! Words like "fear-based" pop up when there's a mention of needing additional funds, and perish the thought of charging big fees for value-based events! Prosperity gurus harp on how money is more than things, while teaching people how to fill their Vision Boards with pretty images of all the "stuff" they desire! Money is the one issue that creates the most disturbing conversations and reactions in board rooms and prosperity classes around the country!

This is where we invite you to take a deep breath, while we emphasize the difference between prosperity and money! Prosperity is a way of thinking, being, and doing, and not just about money and material things. Poverty is a way of thinking, being, and doing, and not just about a lack of money or material things. Both are measured by the degree to which you experience health, happiness, inner peace, and financial freedom. These four lifestyle focus areas are the higher consciousness benefits you'll receive when you attain YOUniversal Prosperity, which happens when you align your Human and Divine Natures. So yes, prosperity is so much more than money!

But think about it! Money *is* one of the main 'prosperity currencies' of the human experience, along with health, happiness, and inner peace. It is the main form of exchange for goods and services in this realm we have decided to inhabit during our skin-school experience. It is critical to have a grasp of how it works and how we use the energy of money to live the abundant life we desire and deserve.

The thing is, most people – New Thought people included – have some difficulty achieving lasting health, happiness, inner peace, or managing money as well as they'd like! The energy of money underwrites all of the world's economies! Yet so many of us do not understand the principles of how the energy of money works in this skin school experience.

The reality is that for many households the world over, the monthly paycheck is barely enough to cover the bills. Nearly 60% of people surveyed over the last 200 years live paycheck-to-paycheck. Most don't have enough cash to cover unexpected costs, such as auto repair, heating and air, and medical bills. Needless to say, saving for something as far off as a six month reserve or retirement or accomplishing other financial goals can feel out of reach. Add something as unexpected and devastating, and an individual's life experience can become traumatizing! If any of this applies to you, you're in good company. In fact, the COVID-19 pandemic of 2020 brought this issue into the bright light of awareness, as millions of people were suddenly thrown into several months of no income, no food, and the threat (often reality) of losing their homes ... not to mention their health.

What has become clear to us is the absolute necessity of fully understanding the laws, principles, and rules about how things work in whatever environment you find yourself. Only when you are armed with this kind of knowledge and insight can you master the art of living in skin school!

Not convinced yet? Consider this: Imagine you are an astronaut who is part of the team traveling to the Space Station. Before you can successfully make the journey, you learn the rules and principles of the new environment you will be entering. You realize gravity operates in a totally different way, which affects how you move, and eat, work and sleep. Your clothing will be different to accommodate the different atmosphere. If you ignored these differences, you would fail miserably at your endeavor ... not because you're not smart enough or committed enough to your dream. You would fail simply because you did not fully comprehend the new and different rules of the world you were entering!

The same is true for working with money here in this realm. We believe it's essential to get a better handle on the importance of money as it relates to your over-all prosperity and to the spiritual practice of a giving consciousness. We need to be able to have conversations about money without guilt, fear, or lack consciousness. We need to be able to link the relationship of health, happiness, inner peace, and money matters so we can truly experience Y☯Universal Prosperity – regardless of what is happening in the world of outer appearances!

The good news is, there are many small steps people can take to stabilize their finances and reach a point where they can save for the long term – and live happily, healthily, prosperously – and achieve lasting inner peace too!

Unfortunately, most prosperity gurus neglect the health, happiness, and inner peace aspects of prosperity – and equate money with prosperity, wrapping their entire shtick around materialistic gratifications like: monetary wealth, success, profitability, affluence, riches, opulence, the good life of material riches, a life of ease and privilege, comfort, security, luxury, a bed of roses, etc. At the same time, they throw in lots of platitudes about it "not being about money" and emphasizing the "this or something better" cliché to justify the situations where their strategies don't produce the desired outcomes! No wonder people come away confused, bewildered, and unfulfilled.

Of course, these prosperity teachers come by it honestly – just not thoughtfully! Most world societies have taught us that prosperity means economic well-being, material riches, political power and privilege, and lots of money. By the way, the etymology of the word 'prosperity' comes from the Latin *prosperitatem* (favorable or fortunate) and '*prosperus*' (good fortune); and from 1200 CE, from the Old French '*prosprete*' and Modern French '*prospérité.*'

The proverbial message is: Success comes from having lots of money and material things. However, a more sane message would be this: Tons of research studies have proven that money, wealth, and material riches don't guarantee lasting happiness unless you have the health, long term happiness, and inner peace that go with it.

So, what's the answer? We believe the answer is uncovering a more realistic definition of prosperity, one that includes money matters, but one that's sooooo much more life-affirming than the materialism and instant gratification bandwagon. We call it Y☯Universal Prosperity!

Take just a moment to re-read our definition of Y☯Universal Prosperity in the first paragraph. In fact, we'll make it easy by including it here again, so you don't have to search it out:

> Y☯Universal Prosperity is *getting your Human Nature in sync with your Divine Nature so you can achieve the Health, Happiness, Inner Peace, and Financial Freedom in less time than you might think, so you can master the art of living in skin school by walking the spiritual path on practical, positive, prosperous feet.*

Y☯Universal Prosperity is defined by five Y☯Universal Prosperity Principles and four important wellness benefits: health matters, happiness matters, inner peace matters, and financial freedom matters. These four lifestyle attributes are the higher consciousness benefits you'll receive when you attain Y☯Universal Prosperity. And how do you attain Y☯Universal Prosperity? We're glad you asked!

We believe you can achieve Y☯Universal Prosperity when you align your Human Nature with your Divine Nature. These two attributes are explained in detail in Part 3 of this book. Both are underwritten by these seven extraordinary abilities:

These are the core abilities that'll make your Y☯Universal Prosperity attainable! Human beings the world over have these seven core abilities and two Y☯Universal Natures (your Human Nature and your Divine Nature) which, when they are aligned, lead to your enlightenment and Self-Realization.

These two Natures are the Y☯Universal Spiritual Duet that makes us truly enlightened beings and they describe what psychologists call our True Self or Authentic Self. We refer to It as our Soul Signature or the Extraordinary Y☯U. Spiritual teachers call It our Higher Spiritual Self, Spiritus, Atman. etc. However, many people fail to align themselves with their Y☯Universal Nature and have no idea how that alignment can help them accelerate their prosperity, let alone achieve full enlightenment and Self-Realization.

You're a very special, very powerful spiritual being who has chosen a human experience. You have many more higher qualities than you think you have. We invite you to try something right now. Read the next paragraph out loud ... as you look at yourself in the mirror. Repeat it again – out loud, with super-high energy and enthusiasm:

I believe in the Extraordinary Me: the Intuitively Wise Me, the Spectacular Me, the Authentic Me, the Phenomenal Me, the Peerless Me, the Exceptional Me, the Unparalleled Me, the Legendary Me, the Marvelous Me, the One-of-a-Kind Me, the Y☯Universally Prosperous Me, the Awesome Me, the Astounding Me, the Stunning Me, the Electrifying Me, the Sensational Me, the Mesmerizing Me, the Amazing Me, the Spellbinding Me, the Hypnotic Me, the Fascinating Me, the Fantabulous Me, the Stupendous Me, the Jaw-Dropping Me, the Mind-Boggling Me, the Dazzling Me, the Brilliant Me, the Compassionate Me, the Kind Me, the Philanthropic Me, the Joyful Me, the Highly Spiritual Me, the Enlightened Me, the Self-Realized Me! I believe in the EXTRAORDINARY ME!

How do you feel after reading this out loud? If it sounds like we're going overboard with those descriptions, we invite you to think for a moment about how much of your hidden potential goes unnoticed, how much of the Real You goes unexpressed. We encourage you to make it a spiritual practice to align your Human and Divine Natures.

Both of these phenomenal Y☯Universal Natures – which we explain in more detail in Part 3 – has four human lifestyle benefits (prosperous states of being) that will help you maximize your skin school (earth) experience. Any one of these prosperity benefits can be enriching in itself. However, achieving all four at the same time would be a wonderful place to be. Don't you agree? We call that 'place' Y☯Universal Prosperity. 'Capital S' Self-Realization (which is conscious oneness with the Extraordinary Y☯U, your Higher Self) is possible when you achieve Y☯Universal Prosperity using what you learn in this cutting-edge book.

In our opinion, achieving lasting health, happiness, inner peace, and financial freedom at the same time is mastering the art of living in skin school! If you establish that kind of alignment every day, you'll enjoy the highest kind of privilege there is – the privilege of being your Authentic Self, the Extraordinary Y☯U, as you live, move, and have your being in skin school!

You'll find the health, happiness, inner peace, and financial freedom you seek when you align your Human Nature with your Divine Nature. And when you do, you'll achieve a 'Soul Signature' that identifies and fosters a higher consciousness vibration of your Y☯Universal Self, which will express itself in whatever dimension of being you find yourself.

Your soul growth status will be greatly enhanced when you get really good at each of these four lifestyle benefits. While we share lots of Y☯Universal Prosperity tips in the following pages, they aren't all-inclusive. That would take thousands of pages. However, what we've provided will be a good start, and perhaps all you'll need as you work toward your own Y☯Universal Prosperity.

Our goal as Unity ministers is to invite you to an uplifting, worldwide spiritual community where you'll feel safe, loved, and respected, so you can master the art of living in skin school by walking the spiritual path on practical, positive, prosperous feet.

Part 1:
Y☯Universal Prosperity Principles

Any systematic approach that's worth its salt is built on basic Principles, defined as the fundamental truths or propositions that serve as the foundation for a system of belief or behavior. (Meriam-Webster). This was literally the #1 frustration that ignited our 5-year deep dive into Prosperity. Our experience was that there were no foundational Principles that were provable, replicable, and scientifically sound. Sure, there were plenty of guidelines and suppositions,; however, we found them sadly lacking when put to the test.

As a result of our research and application results, we have turned seven myths of prosperity on their heads, and transformed them into Seven Y☯Universal Prosperity Principles we would take to the bank! Fasten your seatbelt and get ready for a generous dose of cognitive dissonance (also known as the sound of your mind stretching!) with our myth busting that challenges your deepest-held beliefs about prosperity – what it means and how to achieve it.

Our seven incredible Y☯Universal Prosperity Principles, powered by the MetaSpiritual perspective, which is the spiritual operating system we recommend, will help you align your Human Nature with your Divine Nature so you can master the art of living in skin school. Each Principle enriches those age-old prosperity teachings which were based on old paradigms built on existing knowledge and thought processes of that particular era.

You might be wondering how we came up with these seven Principles. Just so you know, over the past 5 years:

- We've dug into the last 95 years of New Thought prosperity teachings;
- We've spoken to prosperity gurus from New Thought spiritual communities as well as mainstream religious churches;
- We've researched the wealthiest people throughout history as well as those living today – to glean their prosperity wisdom;
- We've explored what neuroscience, psychology, epigenetics, and other sciences have discovered to support the premises of these Principles; and
- We've put each Principle to the test, using it in our own lives to ensure each one is, indeed, a Principle we could present with authenticity and integrity.

As we mentioned in our Introduction, during our 40+-year association with Unity we've got to confess that we've found many of the old prosperity claims were never validated. No matter how well intentioned those claims may have been, they weren't supported by evidence that would confirm their accuracy. Stories used to support Principles could not be validated or replicated. Participants too easily misinterpreted the teachings, and ended up taking actions that led to huge debt incurred, disastrous financial decisions, and even bankruptcy. An abundance of "Metaphysical Malpractice" occurred, resulting in fear and guilt that grew just as strongly as it had in more traditional religious teachings.

If you've attended any of the 'sound too good to be true' prosperity classes, you probably have similar experiences. We believe that if a prosperity principle is based on truth, it should be able to be replicated by everyone.

Of course, prosperity means different things to different people. Dictionaries define prosperity as the state of being very wealthy, of having plenty of money, of having a rich and full life. However, many of the people we've researched believe prosperity means more than that. We've coined a new term to describe our approach to spirituality. We call it a MetaSpiritual perspective, which is the spiritual operating system we incorporate to serve as the marriage between evidence-based science, faith-based spirituality, and metaphor-based metaphysics. When you put those three together, you've just expanded the bandwidth of your consciousness.

And it's that perspective that helps determine fact from fiction, and Truth from dogma. It may surprise you to know that many people question their worthiness to prosper. No matter what mainstream faith tradition we've grown up in, most of us have been taught how unworthy we are, how sinful we are. Here's our answer to the unworthiness issue:

Take a deep breath. You're about to hear what we consider to be the founding principle for our life work. It's about humankind's relationship with GOD (Global Omnipresent Divinity) and how that relationship guarantees our collective worthiness … and lays the groundwork for achieving Y☯Universal Prosperity. Are you ready? Okay! Here it comes:

> *We are … you are … everyone is the individualized Life Force of GOD (Global Omnipresent Divinity), the Image of GOD, actualizing through our Divine Nature as us in human form. In our opinion, that's what's meant by 'we are made in the image of GOD.' This individualized Life Force is our Soul Signature, our Spiritual IP Address. It's our timeless Personal Identity in the Cosmos.*

That's why we believe our loved ones recognize us and we recognize them in the afterlife! It could very well be why people believe we've been together before in a past life. We believe understanding that Ultimate Truth is one of the keys to becoming consciously one with your Divine Nature! It's your superhighway to YOUniversal Prosperity in skin school!

Have you ever played Peek-a-Boo with a child? It's kind of fun, for about 2 minutes! But take a tip from us. Don't ever play Peek-a-Boo with a child sitting in front of you on an airplane – especially if you're traveling non-stop from the east coast to Los Angeles! It becomes tiring – then frustrating – and finally just plain annoying!

That's how it was feeling to us as we were practicing the Prosperity Principles we'd been taught – and that we taught to others! Sometimes it looked like it was working ... other times not! Sometimes we could see it – other times we could not!

Recently during a Sunday talk, we posed a question to the congregation – and we asked them to be completely honest with us! We asked for a show of hands, no guilt intended, indicating how many of them have said, at some point along their spiritual journey, "I'm doing all the right stuff! Why aren't these principles working for me?" As we encouraged them to keep their hands up – we invited them to look around the room – not at individual faces, but at the number of hands up! We thanked them for their honesty, because there were a lot of hands raised – including ours! How about you? Would your hand be raised? You are not alone! It's time to acknowledge the Truth: Something's been left out of the formula! It's time to stop playing Peek-a-Boo with Prosperity! We literally stopped teaching prosperity until we felt we had a handle on what the REAL Principles were, and could share them with integrity and experience!

We've grounded our new approach to prosperity in the teaching of Jesus, from John 10:10. He said, "I have come that you might have life and have it more abundantly!" MetaSpiritually this tells us that we have ready access to the Field of Infinite Potential! And when we align our Human Nature with our Divine Nature, we experience what we call Y☯Universal Prosperity: harmony at the highest level of health, happiness, inner peace, and financial freedom. When these four areas are in harmony, we get that uninterrupted flow. Once we realized this Truth, we started exploring the traditional Prosperity teachings one at a time, to reframe them as Y☯Universal Prosperity Principles.

Ours isn't a YOYO prosperity perspective: YOYO, meaning You're On Your Own prosperity perspective. So we provide a variety of recommendations, tips, science, and spiritual practices throughout this book that show you how you can become as prosperous as you want to be. You can depend on that.

All right! Fasten your seatbelts and let's get started! In order to master Y☯Universal Prosperity, we believe it is critical for you to understand and embrace seven key Y☯Universal Prosperity Principles that are the basis for our prosperity message. Here they are in a nutshell, followed by a detailed description of each one that includes the Prosperity Myth it is busting. First, the Principles:

1. **Y☯Universal Prosperity Principle of the Giving and Receiving Cycle:** Giving increases your consciousness of abundance because 'The Indwelling Truth Harmoniously Increases Never-Ending Good.'

2. **Y☯Universal Prosperity Principle of Positive Affirmations:** Things don't become true because we affirm them. We affirm things because they are grounded in Universal Truths.

3. **Y☯Universal Prosperity Principle of Uninterrupted Flow:** Our Good comes THROUGH us as we Divinely Order our Greater Good.

4. **Y☯Universal Prosperity Principle of Mind Action:** Thoughts held in mind with feeling and emotion produce more thoughts of the same kind.

5. **Y☯Universal Prosperity Principle of Manifesting Our Good:** Intention (Focus) plus Actions in alignment with that intention produce Manifestation.

6. **Y☯Universal Prosperity Principle of Faithing It Till You Make It:** We can call forth the Inner Strength and resilience we need, the Intuitive Wisdom, and our dominion over the world of outer appearances when we have a strong faith-based belief system.

7. **Y☯Universal Prosperity Principle of Doing What You Love: Do What You Love and Life Satisfaction, Joy, a Sense of Fulfillment, Enduring Happiness, a Respectable Livelihood, Contentment, and Inner Peace Will Follow!** If what you love provides you with the financial security to continue doing what you love, enjoy it all the more. And if doing what you love doesn't quite provide enough money, be open to a variety of income streams that'll help support your doing what you love, so you won't have to worry about money matters at all.

We believe in these principles! We know they work! Why? Because we've studied over 100 prosperous people throughout history like: Bill Gates and Warren Buffett, Suze Orman and Marsha

Sinetar, the 14th Dalai Lama and Thich Nhat Hanh, Dave Ramsey and Howard Schultz, Catherine Ponder and Mute-cha Prada, Charles and Myrtle Fillmore, Eric Butterworth and Emilie Cady, Steve Jobs and Andrew Carnegie, Louise Hay and John D. Rockefeller, Jakob Fugger and Henry Ford, to name only a few. These Principles worked for them, and they will work for you! You just need to believe you deserve to be prosperous – believe you deserve to experience abundant health, happiness, inner peace, and financial freedom!

Let's dive more deeply into these Seven Y☯Universal Prosperity Principles, along with each overly popularized prosperity myth we are questioning, and how we're redefining it so you can see the science and spirituality that underwrite each Principle we are celebrating. As you study these Y☯Universal Prosperity Principles, and begin integrating them into your life, we believe you will see their power and experience the excitement of being able to replicate prosperity manifestation into all areas of your life, resulting in the highest, most elevated levels of Health, Happiness, Inner Peace, and Financial Security. So take a deep breath … we'll wait! Now, let's go for a deep dive into Y☯Universal Prosperity Principles.

Questioning Some Myths — and Replacing Them With 21st Century Y☯Universal Prosperity Principles

Myth #1: Tithe 10% and you will receive a ten-fold return. You can't outgive God!

Truth #1: Y☯Universal Prosperity Principle of the Giving and Receiving Cycle: Giving increases your consciousness of abundance because 'The Indwelling Truth Harmoniously Increases Never-Ending Good.'

The Tithing and 10-Fold Return Myth creates a sense of entitlement, along with feelings of confusion and a consciousness of lack. 'Giving to get' tightens the reins of free-flowing abundance in all areas of your life!

A giving consciousness means having an open palm instead of a closed fist. A giving consciousness means realizing that your personal and professional success and happiness are never more than a thought or act of generosity away.

Neuro-biologically speaking, a giving consciousness is nestled within the same frontal regions of the brain that are activated by awe, wonder, joy, and transcendence. An internal coherence results, which fortifies your immune system, strengthens the neural pathways in the frontal lobe, and arrests the feelings of fear and uncertainty which are the products of the amygdala.

A giving consciousness is one of your deepest connections to your Extraordinary Self. It acknowledges your oneness with and appreciation for the Authentic You. It's the realization that there is more to you than any of the circumstances you face. It's the recognition that you have a capacity to give that outshines any thoughts of lack.

It's one of the seven core abilities that characterize your Divine Nature. Research at the University of California, San Diego and Harvard University provides laboratory evidence that giving behavior spreads between people. Those who benefit from kindness tend to find it contagious – and "pay it forward" by helping others.

James Fowler, an associate professor of political science at UC San Diego, and Nicholas Christakis, a Harvard sociology professor, showed that when one person gave money in a 'public-goods game' to help others, the recipients were more likely to give money away in the future. The domino effect continued as more people were swept up in the tide of kindness and cooperation.

From an awareness of plenty, give from the unique and incredible gifts you have. Notice that when you give freely, you're operating from the Principle of the Giving and Receiving Cycle. Spiritual prosperity flows back and forth in a way you can bank on!

It's not about claiming a tenfold return, a hundred-fold return, or simply some kind of a return. Why? ***Because expecting something in return when we give something to someone isn't a consciousness of giving. It's a consciousness of entitlement.*** Expecting something in return denies the ever-present availability of Universal Substance which you can manifest anytime you want through your own connection with your Divine Nature.

Giving from a generous spirit comes from that place in you that recognizes you are connected with Divine Substance, and have access to all you ever need. Live from this spirit. Allow yourself to be generous in whatever ways you can. Remember, it's not about the amount you're able to give – it's about the attitude from which you're giving. Whether it's money, time, support, hope, joy – the underlying value is about your generous spirit.

Here are some characteristics of people who understand the Giving and Receiving Cycle:

- **They give to give; they don't give to get:** They aren't generous in order to impress others or broadcast how much money or food or time they donate or how impressive their works of service are. They generally give quietly and humbly. Generous people don't wait for opportunities for generosity to come to them. They seek out ways they can help others. They know that some of the most needy people will never approach another person for assistance. So, generous people take the initiative when it comes to giving so they can lift the self-esteem of others instead of making someone feel inferior or unworthy.
- **They generate an atmosphere of hospitality and caring by having a warm and inviting spirit about them:** They understand that sometimes even the best of intentions and circumstances conflict, and that they can't be all things to all people at all times. However, they send out an energy of caring, compassion, caring, and harmony, regardless of the situation. Generosity is such an integral part of who they are that they do not expect any praise.
- **They see giving as an investment in the mutual happiness of both the giver and receiver:** Their passion for generosity energizes and revitalizes them to be even more generous. Highly generous spiritual people realize that you can't offer your generosity too soon, because you never know how soon it could be too late for someone needing but not receiving a generous act.

- **They see the currency of generosity as a priceless gift:** Spiritual people with a selfless generous spirit know that acts of genuine generosity raise levels of happiness, emotional well-being, contentment, and a deepening of the sense of oneness and community. They don't measure generosity by the size of the gift, but by the size of the giver's consciousness. Consistent givers structure their lives in ways that make generosity more spontaneous, fulfilling, and fun.
- **They understand the Zen concept of non-attachments:** Practicing generosity helps condition the mind in a way conducive to attaining enlightenment. By that we mean giving serves as a way to eliminate one's selfishness and desire for unnecessary attachments. By giving away what's valuable, generous spiritual people reduce any need for over-consumptive attachments by letting them go. By using possessions or time to benefit someone else, they reinforce their altruism towards others. Giving helps to rid their mind of materialism by conditioning the mind to let go of unnecessary material things. On another note, generous givers are able to give freely, with no attachment to how their gifts are used. They give with no expectation of something in return.

While we are talking about this Principle, we'd like to address the idea of tithing. Without going into all the history behind the tithing requirement that seems to be embedded into every prosperity class and book we studied in the past, we want to go on record saying it is time to let go of the tithing concept as a rule to give 10% (gross or net is still up for clarification!) to the source of your spiritual enrichment, in order to receive a 10-fold return. This whole teaching screams of entitlement: I give to get; I track what comes back; I give with strings attached, and an expectation of a 10-fold return. It defies everything we've just shared about a giving consciousness!

However, we found the word Tithing to be so ingrained in people's consciousness it was nearly impossible for them to let it go! So we created an acronym for TITHING that more appropriately reflects our spiritual understanding of a Giving Consciousness:

The
Indwelling
Truth
Harmoniously
Increases
Never-ending
Good

Myth #2: Affirm it and it will manifest. Corollary: Be careful what you ask for and how to word it.

Truth #2: Y☯Universal Prosperity Principle of Positive Affirmations: Things do not become true because we affirm them. We affirm things because they are grounded in Truth.

Think about that myth for a minute! It sounds great, and has inspired many people to craft beautifully-worded affirmations designed to cover all the bases. It has led to numerous guilt trips and metaphysical malpractice when someone does not get what they affirmed and are told it was because they didn't "ask right!" Award-winning books and movies (you know which ones we're talking about!) have touted this myth to the point that people actually believe they can affirm a million dollars and it will appear on their doorstep! We say, "Seriously? Get over it!" It's time to speak the truth about affirmations! Let's begin with a question:

Do you talk to yourself? Do you talk to yourself out loud? Now for the totally revealing question: Do you answer yourself? (We believe those who answer affirmatively are the truly sane people … they know a good conversationalist when they find one!)

Seriously, research says we all talk to ourselves – and 75-95% of what we say is usually negative. Does that surprise you? Take a few moments to consider how you talk to yourself. Conduct a little personal inventory, reviewing your self-talk. What percentage is positive? How much of what you say is criticism about yourself?

If you have used self-demeaning comments to describe yourself, it's time to re-program your messages. What you tell yourself has a direct relationship on your ability to handle stress; deal with people; achieve personal, professional, and spiritual goals; and connect with your Higher Self.

We unabashedly advocate selling yourself on yourself. And the secret behind this Y☯Universal Prosperity Principle lies in what you are affirming. Too many times we spout mindless affirmations claiming the manifestation of some material thing. But remember this Principle: *We affirm things because they are grounded in Truth!* That means we need to delve more deeply into the essence of what it is we are affirming, and identify the Truth that underwrites it. Develop a set of short, powerful, positive affirmations about yourself that are grounded in Truth. We call them PETs: Personal Empowerment Triggers. Here are a few examples:

- I am one with the Inexhaustible Source of my abundant supply and I am blessed with awesome prosperity.
- I am one with the Eternal Presence and I have such *heir* power that I attract and enjoy unlimited abundance.
- Because I am one with my Higher Self, I enjoy peace, health, and plenty in all areas of my life.
- I am one with Infinite Intelligence and I live joyfully and prosperously at the speed of my Divine Nature.

We invite you to create PETs of your own. A few rules are in order as you prepare your PETs:

1. **Keep your PETs positive and life-affirming.** Instead of saying things like, "*I am no longer tired,*" say, "*I am filled with vibrant energy.*"

2. **Keep PETs in the present tense.** Avoid phrases like "*I'm going to be able to speak in public with confidence someday*" or "*I intend to be more successful at living the truth principles I know.*" Instead, give yourself positive launches like "*I speak in front of groups with ease and*

confidence" or *"I am living the truth principles I know joyfully and successfully every day."*

3. **Repeat your PETs several times a day, with enthusiasm and energy!** Visualize yourself as if these affirmations are already manifest in your life.

4. **Develop three types of PETs:**
   - One set includes a core curriculum of short, go-to statements you can call on at any time to affirm the Truth of who you are – PETs that are related to your general attitude, philosophy, and well-being (*I am one with my Divine Nature, and I am rich, healthy, and happy in all areas of my life*).
   - The second type relates to specific spiritual goals (*I live a Truth-centered life. I align my Human Nature with my Divine Nature, my True Self, with speed, ease, comfort, and joy. I am a Field of Infinite Potential and joyfully manifest work that uses my gifts and supports my preferred lifestyle.*)
   - The third are what we like to call the **"Secret Sauce!"** These are the affirmations that seem to defy all the "rules" you've been taught ... and yet, these are the ones we have found most powerful! They are longer, and follow a specific structure. Let's share an example first, and then break down the structure. This affirmation is geared around health: *I have now transcended all patterns of pain and illness. I am free and healthy! My mind and my body now manifest Divine perfection. I love and accept my body completely. I am good to my body and my body is good to me. I give thanks for ever-increasing health, beauty, and vitality. I am a radiant actualization of uninterrupted health.*

The Secret Sauce Structure for Powerful Affirmations

Now let's break it down into the Secret Sauce Structure for Powerful Affirmations! We'll use an affirmation written for Prosperity as the example here. You'll recognize the similar pattern to the example above.

DENIAL FOLLOWED BY AFFIRMATION STATEMENT	I have now transcended all patterns of lack and limitation. I am healthy, peaceful, happy, and prosperous!
STATEMENT OF TRUTH PRINCIPLE	Prosperity flows through me easily and effortlessly, and I have plenty of resources to share and to spare.
STATEMENT OF FAITH	I stand in the Field of Infinite Potential, knowing I can manifest whatever I need to fulfill my purpose and my dreams.
STATEMENT OF ACTION	I claim my Core Abilities and Spiritual Powers at their highest and most elevated levels in order to wisely use my resources for the good of all concerned.
STATEMENT OF GRATITUDE & REAFFIRMATION OF THE TRUTH OF WHO I AM	I give thanks for ever increasing prosperity and health in all areas of my life! I AM a prospering expression of the Omnipresent Universal Consciousness … and I AM Extraordinary!

Take a few minutes to either write a couple of PETs or revamp a few of your favorite affirmations based on the "rules" we've shared. We invite you to use the above formula to create one powerful Secret Sauce Affirmation in an area of your life you really want to focus on. Then keep it where you will see it – and repeat it aloud – several times a day! (Go ahead and take care of that before you continue!)

How did it feel to write, modify, and speak your PETs? Most people admit that after the initial awkwardness of saying positive things about themselves disappears, this activity feels pretty good.

Record your PETs as a message to yourself on your smart phone, as an mp3, or on a CD. Be as up-beat and enthusiastic as possible. Then, on your way to and from work or when you're running errands, call up your message and play it over and over! Reinforce your success with your own personalized *sell yourself on yourself* pep talk.

Don't feel frustrated if you don't believe yourself initially. When you get serious about something, self-doubt tends to creep in just a little. After all, you may have accumulated a lifetime of negative self-talk. **The important thing to remember about affirmations is that you're not saying affirmations to make them true, you're affirming them because they're grounded in Universal Truths.**

We recommend two extraordinary practices for you to adopt. One is what we call an 'Affirmation Sandwich.' Anytime you're sensing yourself feeling *out of whack* – stuck in a *diddlysquat order kind of experience* – pause and take a few  moments in the Silence; then grab a notepad or your journal and write the alphabet down the left hand side of the page.

Then, for each letter of the alphabet, brainstorm positive, powerful, even spiritual words. For example, for A you might use Awesome or Authentic; B could be Brave or Blessed; C might be Creative or Caring. Then create affirmations, using the words you selected by placing "I am ..." in front and at the end of them – which is, you guessed it – an Affirmation Sandwich! For example, I Am Awesome, I Am; I am Brave, I Am; I am Creative, I Am ... (By the way, this is particularly effective when you're stuck in traffic! Simply look at the license plates on the cars around you, and come up with positive words for the letters on those plates! Honest – it is transforming!)

The second practice is an invitation to 'Take the Fillmore Challenge:' Unity's co-founder, Myrtle Fillmore said: *"Never make an assertion, no matter how true it may look on the surface, that you do not want to see manifest in your life."* Think about this phrase. It forces you to be really aware of what you're saying. Even something as simple as "I am so tired." Or "I'm having a bad hair day." You don't want to see those things manifest, so don't say them!

And by becoming aware of what you're saying, you're also becoming aware of what you're thinking! So we invite you to make the Fillmore Challenge a habit, don't "... make an assertion, no matter how true it may look on the surface, that you don't want to see manifest in your life." And if you catch yourself saying something that's not the Truth of who you are - simply acknowledge what you're feeling (it's okay to admit it!), then affirm your choice to let it go (*refuse to give it any more power!*), and immediately replace what you said with a new, strong, powerful I AM statement that reflects the Truth of who you are! And notice the transformation in your energy, your attitude, and your experience!

"I AM" – two simple, but powerful soul defining words – They launch a powerful vocal vibration that holds the key to unbelievable spiritual growth that leads to your ability to Divinely

Order your experience. And remember what a beautiful spiritual being you really are … as you master the art of living, by walking the spiritual path on practical, positive, prosperous, and affirmation-conditioned feet!

Myth #3: Our good comes to us, and we trust Divine Order to bring us that good.

Truth #3: Y☯Universal Prosperity Principle of Uninterrupted Flow: Our Good comes THROUGH us as we Divinely Order our Greater Good.

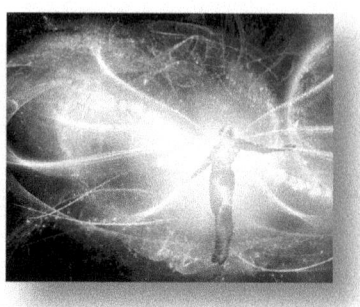

Experiencing flow is a concept coined by Hungarian psychologist Mihaly Csíkszentmihályi to refer to experiences in which there's total, focused concentration and complete involvement in an activity. In his seminal work, *Flow: The Psychology of Optimal Experience*, Csíkszentmihályi outlines his theory that people are happiest when they are in a state of *flow*.

It's a state of such intense involvement and absorption that people say nothing else matters. Athletes say it's being *in the zone* or *in the groove*. Mystics and spiritual teachers describe it as being in *ecstasy*. Artists, dancers, and musicians call it *aesthetic rapture*. It's defined as an optimal state of intrinsic motivation, where someone is fully immersed in what he/she is doing.

You've probably been 'in the zone' or 'in the flow' at times, especially when you were completely involved in an activity for its own sake. You've no doubt felt the pull of great absorption, engagement, fulfillment, and even superior skill – during which all of your temporal concerns (time, food, egocentric appetites and wants, etc.) were typically ignored. Your sense of ego falls away. Every action you take and movement you make seem to be in sync and effortless.

The key aspect to flow is control, according to Csíkszentmihályi, who says, "In the flow-like state, we exercise control over the contents of our consciousness rather than allowing ourselves to be passively determined by external forces." This is completely the opposite of what Prosperity Myth #3 advocates. Believing we are dependent on some outside force sending us our good, and labeling anything that happens as "Divine Order" puts us in a state of victim consciousness and lacking the self-reliance that is at the core of our being.

Understanding the concept of flow affirms that we can create a 'symbiotic dance' between intrinsic and extrinsic activities. Why? Because we're the intersection between Spirit and matter, wave states and particle states, the Tao and the world!

As the Father of Positive Psychology, Martin Seligman, puts it, "Consciousness and emotion are there to correct our trajectory; when what we're doing is seamlessly perfect, we don't need them."

So, when it comes to your prosperity, do you want a sharp edge working for you or a dull edge? A sharp edge is a dependable cutting edge. Any good cook and craftsperson will tell you that a dull edge will cause trouble. A dull edge is not a working edge. It takes too much effort and the results are usually disappointing.

If you're not as prosperous as you think you could be, this Y☯Universal Prosperity Principle invites you to defriend the dull edges in your life! The dull edges we're talking about are things like doubt, fear, feelings of unworthiness, negativity, an unforgiving heart, dogma, the embedded theology you grew up with, and denying your innate divinity!

Here's the secret to prosperity shaping: your prosperity comes *through* you! You can affirm all you want, storyboard all you want, visualize all you want, pray and meditate 24-7, and act as if the objects of your desires are already here; however, if you put your human ego ahead of your Divine Nature, if you fail to forgive, or if you neglect your giving consciousness, you will dam up the flow.

Many people think your good comes *to* you – from out there. From a worldly perspective everything seems to come from 'out there.' And that's the mindset most people have because they've been taught that an anthropomorphic God with human qualities is 'out there' separate from them.

They've been taught that they must petition an absent deity for the things they want. They've been programmed to believe that they've got to be good or they won't get the things they want from the goodie god humankind has created in its image. Is any of this sounding familiar?

When you realize that your good comes *through* you, you'll experience the prosperity you seek! When you realize that your good comes *through* you, you'll hear that 'still small voice.' When you realize that your good comes *through* you, you'll weather any economic conditions and emotional storms with confidence, grace, and poise because you'll know you 'prosperity shape' from the inside out!

Prosperity shaping means filling your consciousness with more prayer, meditation, metaphysical studies, positive affirmations, and over-all positivity. It gets you past the 'LULL' of attraction so that there's no 'LULL' between manifesting something and waiting for what you want to manifest.

Whenever you consciously engage in an activity – any activity – you develop a concentrated flow to such an extent you are able to turn every potential move, thought, and action into an enjoyable experience, and thereby maintain a state of inner tranquility as a continuous and focused state of mind.

Mix physical activity with concentrated spiritual energies as you teach yourself to become immersed. Pay attention to what's happening – what you're creating – in the moment. Proportion your skills to the work at hand. Enjoy the immediate feedback that you're so thoughtfully orchestrating. Recognize that the flow state is a dynamic rather than static state, since a properly constructed flow activity leads to increased skill, challenge, intuitions, and superior focus over time.

Csíkszentmihályi recounts research on the amount of information the brain can process at a time, and points out the constant tradeoffs you'll make about what you're paying attention to out of the infinite number of possibilities available. You'll discover one key aspect of flow is that, while in flow, nearly all of your brain's available inputs are devoted to the activity you're focused on.

This is why your perception of time changes, discomfort goes unnoticed, and stray negative thoughts don't enter your mind. Your brain is too busy focusing on your 'critical one thing' to keep track of all those other distractions.

We see here an obvious link between flow and the Buddhist concept of mindfulness. One of the chief characteristics of your flow state is achieving *moksha* (liberation from the egocentric self), which combines three main intrinsic qualities: expanded beingness, elevated consciousness, and bliss – all of which are very high spiritual qualities.

You'll find that even in a 'simple' flow state, your spiritual growth and even enlightenment are a matter of emancipating yourself from the power of your sense-addicted, worldly-attached ego. Enjoy being *'in the flow'* or *'in the zone'* or *'in the groove'* or *'rapturous'* or *'ecstatic.'* This is a Y☯Universal Prosperity Principle you'll want to replicate many times because it helps you to Divinely Order your Greater Good!

A Little Background on the Religious Concept of Divine Order – From Our Perspective:

Most dogmatic religions define 'divine order' in much the same terms as they describe their relationship with the God of their faith tradition. For the religious, it seems to be based on the Biblical notion of divine order: "Not my will, but Thy will be done" (Luke 22:42).

The religious faithful believe that no one is entitled to rearrange God's divine order. So, they trust what they believe to be the divine flow of the Lord's plan and follow it without question. It's a docile perspective. The secret to happiness is believed to lie in the maintenance of a pre-determined divine order, or confusion and discord will be the result.

We have a different interpretation of Divine Order, as you may have guessed, based on a MetaSpiritual perspective. Divine Order, in our opinion, isn't an external God-generated fiat or something a celestial deity imposes upon us. Divine Order isn't an event. It's a process. It's not a pre-determined outcome and it's certainly not a pre-emptive course of action on our part, as spiritual beings in human form, to manifest something visible from the invisible.

Divine Order is an intentional creative process of Mind-Idea-Expression, which is an exceptional process of creating something we desire by right of consciousness. We can be in the Flow and *Divinely Order* good, or we can be out-of-sync and misapply the Mind-Idea-Expression process, creating error expressions. A Divine Idea can be expressed spiritually or selfishly. Spiritually expressed, it's capital "D" Divine Order. Selfishly expressed, it's what we call 'diddlysquat order,' since a Divine Idea has been misapplied.

Divine Order occurs when we Divinely Order our experience from the consciousness of our oneness as the human expressions of the One Reality, the Global Omnipresent Divinity. *Diddlysquat order* is a millstone perspective. It means allowing our unenlightened ego to tempt us into believing we're separated from the One Reality that underwrites our existence, that we're not divine beings, and that all good things must come to an end. What we need to remember most is that when we're in the Flow, we're always Divinely Ordering our human experience. There's always an order to what we're doing! We just don't always use it at our highest, most elevated level of expression.

Divinely Ordering our good is a conscious process of allowing our prosperity to flow *through* us. It's affirming our Greater Good. It's recognizing that Divine Substance is available to us each-consecutive-moment-of-now!

Myth #4: Thoughts held in mind produce after their kind.

Truth #4: Y☯Universal Prosperity Principle of Mind Action: Thoughts held in mind with feeling and emotion produce more thoughts of the same kind.

This prosperity myth permeates everything that is taught about prosperity, and has become such an iconic belief that we get bombarded with cries of dismay when we call it a myth! And we'll admit it holds a grain of Truth. The problem is, it is  so misunderstood. People tend to interpret this as saying if I think it, it will show up! Seriously? Can you imagine what a mess our lives would be if every thought we held in our mind actually manifested?

Here's the reality. We have many thoughts during the course of a day. Some thoughts 'drive by' like the vehicles we see on highways. Others linger or even repeat themselves. The important thing you need to know about thoughts is that your thoughts determine your inclinations, your inclinations lead to choices, and your choices lead to actions.

Thoughts and emotions don't happen in a vacuum. You choose them! They are internal reactions to an outside stimulus. You choose to get angry or irritated or impatient. When you are fearful, you choose to be fearful. If you are envious, you choose to be envious. If you are joyful, you choose to be joyful.

The thing about thinking is, every thought you have either honors your *authentegrity* (our mashup word which includes both authenticity and integrity) or multiplies illusion. 'Thoughts held in mind produce after their kind' is a commonly-used expression by many New Thought people. The question is, however: What *kind* of thoughts produce *what* after their kind? The answer seems obvious, but we're going to say it anyway, because it is our Y☯Universal Prosperity Principle of Mind Action: Thoughts held in mind *with feeling and emotion* produce *more thoughts* of the same kind.

That is, they lead to thoughts which are characteristic of the consciousness which spawned them in the first place. This is critically important, so listen up! That means that similar thoughts repeated often enough with feeling and emotion reinforce truth or perpetuate error. What you keep feeding in attracts more thoughts, and as a result, more feelings, of the same kind!

That's how thoughts travel through your mind and that's how thoughts are "auctioned" too! When you control your thinking, you control your thoughts. If you auction your thinking to the world of outer appearances, you auction your life to the world of *wish*craft, quick fixes, and 'too good to be true' schemes.

A Little Science to Support the Y☯Universal Prosperity Principle of Mind Action

In a remarkable scientific breakthrough, researchers at Berlin's Bernstein Center for Computational Neuroscience were the first to measure intentions we hold in our mind *before* the intentions are put into action. For example, when new information enters our brains, they say, it enters into our short-term memory field. The process is called *synaptic transmission*. The electro-chemical impulses ignite one neuron, which in turn ignites another neuron.

The new information is remembered only if the second neuron repeats the impulse back again to the first. This most likely happens when we decide that the new information is important. Affirmations are a perfect example of this repeat firing process.

If the neural 'echo' is sustained long enough, it amps up the brain's incredible neuroplasticity, which leads to lasting structural changes. This 'echo' hard wires the new information, forming memory grooves in your gray matter. That's why it's so important to think positive thoughts, watch positive TV shows, YouTubes, and Internet programs, and play nonviolent games.

If you hard-wire your thoughts only on what you see through the filters of your physical senses, you may create grooves of materiality in your consciousness which make it harder for you to see lasting happiness and success. You'll stop being robbed of your potential successes, which are all around you, when you get really good at doing three things:
- affirming your incredible, extraordinary awesomeness;
- forgiving anyone you believe may have injured or harmed you in any way;
- and expressing your Higher Spiritual Nature every chance you get.

When you do those three things, you'll turn unwanted *mind auction* into positive *mind action*. It's so important to recognize when you are auctioning your thinking! And this self-defeating auctioning process is easy to see! Be on the lookout for these symptoms of mind auction:
- allowing your schedule to rob you of your inner focus time.
- affirming you are a positive person, and then having hour-long discussions with friends about how horrible the economy is, or how helpless you are, or how unworthy you are, etc.
- slipping into old habits of doubt, fear, or just plain give-up-ness.
- reliving hurts caused by someone close to you, and wanting to wear 'staying hurt' as a badge of honor.
- allowing excuses to take the place of healthy life styles.

- sitting back, hoping things will improve, but feeling stuck like a hamster in a cage, running in circles on the wheel!
- thinking this mind action stuff doesn't work – just because you haven't gotten results yet.
- compromising your 'Authentegrity' (that's our mashup word again, that combines authenticity and integrity) by neglecting to align yourself with your Higher Spiritual Nature.

Moving from Mind *Auction* to Mind *Action* takes diligent awareness and a personal commitment to standing in the truth of who you are and practicing the Truth principles you know! It means paying attention to all thoughts held in mind with feeling that are floating in and out of your consciousness, and stop auctioning off the better parts of you!

Myth #5: If you dream it and believe it, you will see it in your life.

Truth #5: Y☯Universal Prosperity Principle of Manifesting Our Good: Intention (Focus) plus Actions in alignment with that intention produce Manifestation.

We've already shared our disdain for the underlying premise of Myth #5! When combined with Myth #4, it is at best wishful thinking, and at its worst is a false promise that leaves a lot of people feeling frustrated, guilty, and unfulfilled. **So let's dig into it, and find the real Truth that, in our opinion, is the most powerful Principle we can share! This Principle holds the key to ensuring your success at manifesting the good you so strongly want to Divinely Order in your life!**

You are pre-wired for manifesting your Greater Good. The ability to manifest what you want and need is built into your spiritual DNA. Have faith in your Divine connection. Have faith that your good is only one thought, one affirmation, one choice, and one principled action away.

Virtually all the blocks to your manifesting what you want are rooted in subconscious issues. By definition, you're unaware of things in your subconscious. The only way you become aware of them is when they manifest through your thoughts, words, and actions. So it makes sense to begin to pay serious attention to your thoughts, words, and actions, so you can identify the useless baggage you're carrying around in your subconscious, and get rid of it! And the point of your personal power is in each now moment!

As a matter of spiritual fact, your Greater Good is never more than a thought away! It's closer than the objects that appear in your car rearview mirror. It's as close as your next breath. It's as close as your next thought, intention, word, choice, or action. It's as close as the book you're holding.

If you're having less than perfect experiences in your finances, your relationships, your work, your health, your attitude, your life ~ just know that it's simply an outer manifestation of what's going on in your subconscious. And you have the power to get in there and make a change in this now moment!

You can SAY you believe you live in an abundant universe, that you always have everything you need at the point of need, that there's plenty to share and plenty to spare ... but if your thoughts, choices, and actions don't support and feed those beliefs, you won't see them manifest!

In order to experience the highest and most elevated manifestation of the spiritual laws of prosperity and abundance, you must make conscious choices, with serious intention. This is really important! First you set your intention, then fuel it with positive emotions and feelings. To transform it into manifested reality, you must make choices that lead to actions which are in alignment with that intention!

For example, if you set the intention of manifesting a certain amount of money, but then spend money frivolously on 'dumb stuff,' your actions are not in alignment with your intention. You will not manifest the results you desire.

Just as an aside (an important aside), remember the power of conferring a blessing as you set your intentions. What you bless multiplies and grows. A blessing means to 'confer prosperity upon.' So, you want to bless, confer prosperity upon, what you want to manifest. You have the incredible power to confer prosperity upon everything, everyone, and every circumstance that comes to you —

and in so doing, you create an unending ripple effect of prosperity and abundance.

This particular Y☯Universal Prosperity Principle is so critical to your manifestation success, and when you understand this, you can literally Divinely Order your experience! Unfortunately, many people upset the timing by holding onto their fears, doubts, assumptions, greed, material attachments, unforgiveness, and illusions of an anthropomorphic God 'out there' separate from us who dispenses favors to some and withholds good from others. Let go of those outdated beliefs and walk into the power of who you are as you put this Principle into action!

Myth #6: Fake it till you make it.

Truth #6: Y☻Universal Prosperity Principle of Faithing It 'Till You Make It: Stand in the Faith of the Truth you know, even when you cannot see the outer manifestation of it yet.

The old, conventional prosperity teaching we've replaced is "Fake it 'till you make it." Another correlated phrase is: "Act As If…" While these glib statements are catchy and popular – and over-used – they really are quite misleading, corrosive, and, when you think about it, entirely self-defeating.

When we operate from a "fake it" mentality, we're messing with our authenticity and integrity. When we come from a place of "faking it," or "acting as if," we're fabricating something we haven't legitimately manifested yet, hoping it will suddenly appear. It's not the same thing as visualizing what we want. This ill-advised practice usually takes the form of masquerading and falsifying physical evidence to 'prove' that you've manifested a particular desire.

Going into needless debt, misrepresenting yourself, and creating a false front aren't healthy practices. This counterfeit practice has often led to serious financial trouble, because people interpret "Act as If …" and "Fake it till you make it…" to mean go out and buy that new house or car – the money will come if you take the action! People end up feeling like frauds … and in deeper debt than before!

We have changed it to say "FAITH it till you make it!" This way, we can call forth the Inner Strength we need, the Intuitive Wisdom, the dominion over the world of outer appearances! We can claim the evidence-based Principles we believe, and use them to move forward with confidence and power. Faith – and responsible action – create the open sesame for legitimate manifestation.

An Example from Unity History

There's a wonderful story told about a time when the Unity Movement was in serious financial straits. Bills that had to be paid were piling up, and there didn't seem to be money enough to meet the payroll. The Fillmores called their staff together to pray about the matter. One of the staff said, "Let's pray that the money holds out." "Oh, no," whispered Myrtle Fillmore. "Let us affirm that our faith holds out."

Do you hear the difference? One is coming from fear and a consciousness of lack; but Myrtle recognized the power of claiming Faith – standing in the Truth of knowing that they could use their collective creativity, intelligence, and responsible actions to manifest the funds they needed from the Field of Infinite Potential. The power of that small difference in wording represents a HUGE difference in *authentegrity,* and is the difference between faking it and faithing it! It's the difference in 'peek-a-boo' prosperity and uninterrupted prosperity! So always FAITH it till you make it!

Myth #7: Do what you love and the money will follow.
Truth #7: Y☯Universal **Prosperity Principle of Doing What You Love**: Do what you love, and Enduring Happiness, Life Satisfaction, Joy, a Sense of Fulfillment, Contentment, and Inner Peace Will Follow!

The seventh antiquated prosperity teaching we've altered is "Do what you love, and the money will follow." Our usual questions are:

Does it mean: Do what you love, and substantial money will follow? Or does it mean: Do what you love, and enough money will follow? Or what if it means: Do what you love, and the money will follow ... depending on what you love?

Ask school teachers, social workers, artists, aspiring actors, dancers, and nurses how they feel about livelihood and money!

Money isn't the main qualifier when it comes to doing something you love. But it's in the mix! Money and material things are just energetic expressions of how we've designed our society. Most New Thought prosperity gurus still teach materialism and tenfold returns. They tend to share undocumented claims they think people want to hear.

There may be a kernel of truth in some of their claims. However, based on our research, many claims are exaggerated to sell that particular guru's materialistic prosperity message. When you think about it, traditional New Thought prosperity teachings aren't 'new thought' teachings at all. They're Old Thought teachings dressed in 21st century rhetoric.

Okay. Take another deep breath. Here's our rewrite of this well-worn prosperity teaching: **Do what you love, and enduring happiness, life satisfaction, joy, a sense of fulfillment, contentment, and inner peace will follow! If what you love provides you with the financial security to continue doing what you love, enjoy it all the more. And if doing what you love doesn't quite provide enough money, be open to a variety of income streams that'll help support your doing what you love, so you won't have to worry about money matters at all.**

Part 2:
The 4 Core Benefits of Achieving Y☯Universal Prosperity – and How to Maximize Them

Health, happiness, inner peace, and financial freedom are the core benefits you'll achieve as you seek to master the art of living in skin school by walking the spiritual path on practical, positive, prosperous feet. In this section we offer practical tips, strategies, and practices to help you boost these incredible benefits. We call them Y☯Universal Prosperity Hors d'Oeuvres.

How to Use the Y☯Universal Prosperity Tips in This Section

This section of the book is the one you will want to come back to, over and over, as you put the Y☯Universal Prosperity Principles into practice in your life. We decided to make it simple, by creating very specific, very practical tips related to each of our four focus areas that, together, result in that Y☯Universal Prosperity everyone desires. For each focus area (Health, Happiness, Inner Peace, and Financial Freedom), you will see a series of our specially-created Yin Yang bullets. Each bullet highlights a specific strategy, tip, or inspirational thought related to that focus area. We like to call these our **Y☯Universal Prosperity Hors d'Oeuvres**: MetaSpiritual, allegorical, spiritual, figurative, metaphorical, metaphysical, theosophical, mystical, and anthroposophical thoughts, perspectives, and down-to-earth teachings. Each hors d'oeuvre is a "sound bite" of wisdom, advice, or inspiration that provides the jumping-off point for a deep dive discussion, ending in some sort of action plan on how to build a new or renewed concept, practice, or thought into your spiritual enrichment lifestyle.

Of course, just reading through them will give you a wide variety of inspiration and practical actions you can take to enhance each focus area in your life. But it could easily leave you feeling overwhelmed and clueless about which thing to do. So we have a specific strategy to suggest, to help you get the best results from using this section of the book.

Go ahead and scan through the hors d'oeuvres for a quick overview of what's in store for you there. Then, when you are ready to zoom in and begin working on that particular focus area, follow this action plan:

ACTION! Using the Hors d'Oeuvres

1. Each morning, choose one of the hors d'oeuvres.

   (You can go in order; randomly choose one; drop a coin on the page; select one that is resonating with you; print the pages, cut them into strips with one per strip, and draw one out of a basket; or however you want to choose it. The key is to pick one—just one!)

2. Meditate, using the selected hors d'oeuvre as your focus for the meditation.

3. Journal your thoughts, feelings, a-ha's, and actions you want to take.

4. For the entire day, keep your focus on that hors d'oeuvre, and what came out of your meditation. Continue using that item until you feel 'complete' with it. Then move on to another one.

5. Some of these hors d'oeuvres won't resonate with you (just like some folks love shrimp and others dislike it). Feel free to pick and choose, and ignore the ones you don't like – Guilt Free!

– Health Matters –

The Health Matters we share are about physical, mental, emotional, and spiritual *wellth*. They include: relationship health, self-care health, work-related health, dietary health, news cycle impact health, social media impact health, and significant life events health. Health is so much more than just physical. To feel you are functioning at your peak level of Y☻Universal Prosperity in the area of Health, you want to ensure you are not only physically and mentally healthy; you also want to focus on having healthy relationships; a healthy work environment; a healthy level of media input (including the news you consume; movies and TV shows; Facebook; Twitter; Instagram feeds; books you read; etc.) Your "Filter Bubble" encompasses all the things you allow into it — and you want to be sure you are determining what is included!

Are you ready for some Health-related Y☻Universal Prosperity Hors d'oeuvres? Let's dig in!

- Use both integrative medicine and traditional medical modalities to ensure your health and well-being. At this point in our human evolution, there are benefits in using both medicinal methodologies.

- Nothing tastes as good as health feels. Did we say *nothing*?

- Realize that fear, anger, resentment, worry, greed, bearing false witness, hurtful prejudice, guilt and unforgiveness have absolutely no nutritional value.

- Understand that our Y☯Universal physical health is largely determined by mind over molecules.

- Our subconscious is like our house basement. It warehouses our tendency to store old, repressed life patterns, belief systems, and warped perspectives that can weigh us down if we continue to allow them to inhibit us and squelch our potential. A cluttered and messy basement (our subconscious) symbolizes our need to rid ourselves of stagnant and debilitating emotions, habits, and false assumptions that keep our potential buried and our waking life burdened with defense mechanisms.

- Do you realize that blood cells that rush to a wound site and treat the wound are wonderful paramedics. Recognize that your body has its own paramedics and pharmacy, which on occasion, can use an assist from traditional and integrative medicine.

- Recognize that not taking time for healthy eating today may mean having to make time for illness later.

- Soul care, self-care, and Self-care are absolutely essential for your Y☯Universal health and wellbeing! Make time for all three in your daily routine. (Notice that third one is a 'Capital S Self … your Divine Nature).

- You don't have to suffer from what research calls 'news cycle fatigue.' Studies show that 65-68% of people watching local and national news get upset, irritated, angry, exhausted, and even traumatized from what they see and hear.  **We don't want you to suffer from what we call PTNCD (Post Traumatic News Cycle Discomfort).** Adopt the practice of detoxing yourself from most of the news coverage by limiting the time you spend watching it! Watch just enough to stay informed without exposing yourself to undue negativity. Put time limits on your exposure just like you put portion limits on the amount of food you eat at mealtime!

- We refer to each of our incarnated physical bodies as the somatic vehicles, taxis, and limousines that we inhabit on our way toward enlightenment. Our physical bodies are the price we pay for another skin school experience.

- The bacteria in your gut (gut microbiota) are incredibly important for your over-all health. Consume probiotic foods like: yogurt, sauerkraut, tempeh, kombucha, pickled cucumbers, sourdough bread, olives and bananas. You may want to add probiotic supplements as well.

- As spiritual beings in human form we can choose wholeness instead of negation, faith instead of fear, confidence instead of confusion, victory instead of victimhood, health instead of illness.

- When we cultivate healthy higher consciousness perspective by paying attention to high spiritual teachings and making them practical, we tap into the Extraordinary Us, our Indwelling I Am Nature, our Global Omnipresent Divinity which transforms our human personality into its higher, more spiritual essence.

- It should come as no surprise that error thoughts are mental contaminants. They surface from a consciousness addicted to things that aren't good for you or your soul.

Recognize that what follows 'I am' follows you.

- A genuinely fulfilling and lasting love relationship is available to all of us – if we raise our consciousness above the din of disbelief, above the feeling that it can't happen to us, above the doubt that we can ever experience such a love.
- It doesn't take much of a leap in awareness to realize your 'cellular family' is composed of highly conscious biocellular beings that respond to your thoughts, emotions and behavior. Have no doubt that your 'cellular community' can be your *well*thy BFF.
- Longevity researchers have discovered what they call 'blue zones' (human longevity areas across the globe) where people live long and healthy lives. The lifestyle habits are the same in all of these zones: moderate, daily exercise; sense of life purpose; reduced stress; moderate caloric intake; plant-based diet; moderate alcohol intake (especially wine); close family ties; and a spiritual more than religious perspective.
- Know that to believe in incurable dis-eases is to retail biological suicide. The truth is there are no incurable dis-eases or illnesses, because your body's cellular architecture is underwritten with health and wholeness. It's just that humankind hasn't discovered the cure yet for a specific dis-ease.

- You say tom*A*to, we say to-m**ah**-to. Tomatoes are superstars in the fruit and veggie pantheon. Tomatoes contain lycopene, a powerful cancer fighter. They're also rich in vitamin C. The good news is that cooked tomatoes don't lose their nutritious value or medicinal punch.

- Social media involvement doesn't have to create 'Facebook envy' or 'Twitter anxiety' or 'App disasters.' It's an information and people connection platform that can be either healthy or unhealthy. Make a selfcare decision. Make it a point to engage in healthy media exposures.

- Give zero credibility to stale religious teachings that are based on fear, guilt and shame and someone's world view that's based on resentment, unforgiveness and hatred. Neuroscientists tell us that stressful teachings and personal condemnations like these force you to live in the amygdala, the area in your brain that's responsible for your *fight, flight, freeze, and please responses*, which can be hazards to your health. Instead, pay attention to views that champion positivity, open-mindedness and optimism, which characterize your neocortex, which is the seat of higher conscious thoughts and functioning that lead to overall health and wellbeing. By the way, your vagus nerve (located just below the brain stem and running down the parasympathetic nervous system), along with its neuropeptide partner, oxytocin, is responsible for the *calm-and-connect response* that's every bit as ingrained evolutionarily as your *fight-flight-freeze-please response.*

- Lower your risk for health complications by sitting for shorter periods of time. Stand and stretch and/or walk around a bit every 30-45 minutes. It gets the blood circulating so you can continue to enjoy circulating with family and friends.

- Here are seven love relationship 'vocabularies' that deepen our soulmate intimacy: sincere compliments, mutual encouragement, quality time together, just because gifts, sharing responsibilities, 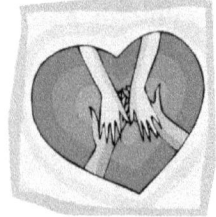 loving and respectful physical contact, and compatibility based on shared curiosity so you grow together and not apart. Which ones are most important to you — both in your relationship with others AND your relationship with yourself?

- Found your relationship on unequivocal unconditional love, indisputable mutual respect and trust, loving memories, romantic moments, laughter and joy, playfulness, respecting your differences, making each other a priority, saying "I love you" every day, and many other soulmate intimacies.

- There's some variance in the number of physical senses that neuroscientists say we humans have, but there's complete agreement that it's many more than the proverbial five physical senses (*sight, sound, taste, smell,* and *touch*). Here are some of the other 25+ 'basic' physical senses we have other than the proverbial five listed above: pressure, sensing time, vibration, pain, skin stretching, textural changes, sense of direction, balance, and so on. We share this with you to show how much more there is to us than meets the eye, ear, nose and throat! Our health depends on all of these physical senses.

- Has it occurred to you that when you take care of your good habits, they'll take care of you?

- Realize that it's the voltage of our faith, or the amperage of our lack of faith, that makes us or breaks us when it comes to our sustained health and wellness.

- Yawn your way to enlightenment! We're serious. Yawning doesn't just relax you - it quickly brings you into a heightened state of awareness. Recent brain-scan studies have shown that yawning evokes a unique neural activity in an area of the brain called the precuneus, a tiny structure hidden within the folds  of the parietal lobe. Neuroscientists tell us that the precuneus plays a central role in consciousness, self-reflection, and memory retrieval. Yawning also cools the brain. So, yawn your way to your over-all health, well-being and enlightenment.

> *For some people a balanced diet is a beer or soda in one hand and a pizza in the other.*

- Suffering is human spiritual unfoldment calibrated to its lowest possible setting. That means the misalignment between our Human Nature and our Divine Nature is what causes suffering. It's the pain and discomfort we experience by not being consciously one with our Higher Self and staying in integrity with our Soul Signature.
- Realize that processed foods generally extend both their shelf life and your waistline.
- Take the following vaccinations – spiritual vaccinations that is! Spiritual vaccinations immunize you from the perceived limitations associated with daily living. Spiritual vaccinations include: affirmative prayers, meditation sessions, positive affirmations, sacred rituals, hugs, spiritual visualizations,

metaphysical study, going to spiritual conferences and retreats, healing sessions, forgiveness, sabbaticals, random acts of kindness, burning bowl celebrations, communing with nature, dancing, walking, jogging, philanthropy, silent relaxation, and taking 365 vacations every year, to name a few. Use all of these inoculations to reinforce your spiritual work. These are all excellent inoculations that'll keep you healthy.

One of the best ways to consistently spend your income wisely is the kind of food and drink you place inside your mouth.

- Don't smoke if you haven't started. And if you smoke already, do everything in your power to kick the habit. In addition to the well-known risks of heart disease and cancer, orthopedic surgeons tell us that smoking accelerates bone density loss and constricts blood flow. Where there's nicotine smoke there's unhealthy fire!
- Recognize that sedentary physical habits lead to sluggish mental habits that inevitably block enlightened thought.
- Affirm confidently: I now transcend all beliefs, patterns, and forms of illness and dis-ease.
- In IT language, malware is short for 'malicious software.' It's software employed to disrupt computer operation, gather sensitive information, or gain access to private computer systems. Malware, MetaSpiritually speaking, is false teachings, anti-enlightenment perspectives, and error-prone tendencies that negatively affect our health and well-being. How can you guard against anti-spiritual malware?

- ☯ Realize that what you eat directly affects your Y☯Universal health and over-all *well*th. A whole-foods, plant-based diet, low-to-no animal protein (5% or less), harmful fats, sugar, and refined carbs is a good lifestyle diet. Too much animal protein significantly decreases blood flow to your brain and heart, and limits the oxygen you need for mental clarity and higher thought. Also, from a physiological health standpoint, a diet high in animal proteins increases the production of debilitating interleukins like IGF-1 which promote chronic inflammations that cause most of our serious illnesses.

> *Talk to your cellular family. It's one of the best relationships for cures. Your cellular community can be your life-long cellular pharmacist.*

- ☯ Blueberries, strawberries and raspberries contain nutrients called anthocyanidins, which are powerful antioxidants. Blueberries have high concentrations of resveratrol – the antioxidant compound found in grapes and red wine that has assumed near mythological proportions. By the way, resveratrol is believed to help protect against heart disease and cancer.

- ☯ Help your brain's neuroplasticity. Researchers have coined the term 'neurobics' for tasks which activate the brain's own biochemical pathways and to bring new pathways online that can help to strengthen and preserve brain circuits. For example, brush your teeth with your 'other' hand, take a new route to work, or choose your clothes based on sense of touch rather than sight. Of course, we believe MetaSpiritually interpreting religious scriptures is neurobic too.

- Some human souls experience a cacophony of jobs and occupations or actual 'callings.' Others graft themselves onto one line of work. Both routes can be spiritual practices. Healthy soul growth comes when there's congruence between who you are and what you do for a living. For some, work itself becomes a sort of morphine. For many, the asphyxia of suffocating work strangles their creativity and self-expression, and steals their health and happiness. Ask yourself: Is it just a way to make ends meet, or is it something more? Is what I do a good match between what I do at work and my skills, talents and values? Does my work sap me or give me energy? Is my work in sync with what I feel a strong inner urge to do as my 'soul' work? Do I see the work I do as a reflection – and particularly an expression – of the choices I've made? Is it connected to me at a soul level? Do I see it as my evolving spirituality made visible?

- Accept who you are and your human worth with a strong inclination toward improving yourself mentally, emotionally, physically, and spiritually.

- Know that the greatest health-related wealth is your over-all *well*th.

- Realize that good-natured laughter is medicinal.

- Our body, coupled with its mental powers and emotional wattage, can become its own pharmacy.

- The greatest wealth is *well*th.

- Watch what you eat and drink so you don't dine beyond your seams!

- Believe this or not, our confidential health advisors can also be pacemakers, glucose monitors, an actual illness or dis-ease, fevers, aches and pains, feelings of 'something not rightness' we get when we listen to our bodies, etc.

- One of the cornerstone foods for healthy longevity is a bean-rich diet. Beans are loaded with protein, iron, zinc, fiber, folate and potassium – and they're low in fat. Consume at least a cup of beans every day.

Our cells, atoms, and molecules are conscious cellular beings. They know when we have their best interests in mind.

- Realize how important physical exercise is and how it can reinforce our body's structural integrity. For example, our quadriceps, buttocks and calves, along with a group of muscles called the erector spinae that surround our spinal column and keep us standing tall, protect us from the pull of gravity that would collapse our human body into a fetal ball and leave it curled on the floor.
- Enjoy brain foods. That just makes good neural sense.
- "We are what we eat" is a familiar saying. However, we believe: we eat based on our evolving preferences and sensory experiences which are based on our Human Nature's habits!
- You're kept in sync or out of sync by the acupuncture of your healthy or unhealthy thoughts, choices, and actions.
- It's very important to remind your significant other how much you appreciate everything he/she does for you. Show your gratitude even for the smallest things. Don't take anything for granted, and let your other half know how special he/she is and that you treasure every single thing in your relationship.
- Listen to your Inner Voice, because It's the Spiritual IV that connects the current human you with your Soul Signature.

- Adopt *alphabiotic thinking* as a regular spiritual healing practice. *Alphabiotic thinking* is the spiritual practice that supports the belief that faith is a necessary condition in the healing process and that all dis-ease is the result of an imbalance and/or blockage in energies essential to health and well-being. The practice of *alphabiotics* is concerned with the damage that unrelieved stress causes to the human body. Much of the stress we experience is caused by our negative reactions to the world of outer appearances. We see the world through the filters of the amygdala and tense up when we feel threatened. It's that very hypertension that blocks our being able to manifest our good from the Field of Infinite Potential. *Alphabiotic thinking*, from a spiritual standpoint, champions the conscious alignment between our body, mind, and soul. It's the kind of thinking that gets us out of the amygdala (our fight, flight, freeze, or pleasse propensity) and into our neocortex (the seat of our higher brain functions). According to Carl Sagan in *Cosmos*, "The neocortex is where matter is transformed into consciousness."

- Adopt the view that the closer your conscious alignment is with your *True Spiritual Nature*, the closer your physical body's connection will be with the species-specific *prana* (Qi attractor) that improves your capacity to resist illness and disease.

- Researchers have found that grip strength is a leading health indicator. Men with a grip strength of 57 lbs have a healthier heart and lungs. For women, grip strength threshold seems to be 35 lbs. Test your grip strength using an analog – not digital – bathroom scale; or the next time you visit your doctor, ask to use their handgrip dynamometer.

- What if acupuncture is a metaphor for aligning the physical us with our Divine Nature?

- In a very real sense, error thinking is usually the result of 'spiritual arrhythmias,' which we believe are the result of irregular or uncharacteristic lapses in following the Truth principles we've learned.

- Work on your balance. The CDC tells us that falls are one of the most over-looked health threats facing older adults that cause disabilities and even death. Soooo, adopt yoga or tai chi for a balancing act. Practice lifting one foot slightly off the floor and then switch after 45 seconds or so, while you're holding lightly onto a table, chair, or countertop.

- Consciousness isn't an epiphenomenal effect of biology. Biology simply records the salient effects of GOD (the Global Omnipresent Divinity, the Omnipresent Ultimate Reality) in the material world (quantum manifold). One day, biologists will see that consciousness is causative and not correlational.

- Be aware that diagnoses can either be medical boundaries maintenanced by fear, shame, or guilt OR catalysts for personal transformation.

- We're not going to gloss over flossing, but flossing doesn't just clean and freshen your teeth. Research shows that periodontal disease can lead to serious and life-threatening health problems. Harmful bacteria can enter the bloodstream, causing serious inflammation which compromises your health and well-being. The Rx is to floss daily.

- Epigenetics research tells us that when we become attuned to our health and wellness that our cells, which are conscious beings, get the message. They defend us from illness and disease and promote our health. We encourage you to add epigenetics to your scientific reading.

- Sometimes an illness reduces us to our fighting weight.

- The higher risk of death has nothing to with the usual heart disease culprits - age, blood pressure, cholesterol, diabetes, excessive weight. Instead, it tracks closely with the power of belief. Think sick, be sick. Think a disease is fatal, and chances are it'll be fatal.

- Recognize that your health doesn't so much depend on unanswered health and well-being questions as it does on questioning unquestioned answers about health-related matters.

- Lift weights first during your workouts. Physiology experts say weight training should be done first, because it's a higher intensity exercise compared to conventional cardio routines. Also, rev up your metabolism by alternating your speed and intensity during aerobic workouts, because it helps prevent burnout and boredom.

- Psychologists have found that a positivity resonance between our thoughts and emotions strengthens our immune system and cardiovascular system and lowers our blood pressure and incidences of inflammation.

- Know that part of a cure is wanting to be cured as well as healed.

- Be aware that many people face a battalion of addictions each day. Some fill their despondency with alcohol. Others elect to diffuse their poor dietary choices with over-the-counter drugs. Some have turned their medicine cabinets into pharmacies. Many are swayed by the pharmaceutical industries propaganda and manipulative advertising to the point that they blindly buy anything "pharmaceutical pied pipers" offer. It takes only one medication to make a person drowsy, forgetful, listless, or semiconscious—but he or she is usually not sure if it's the sixth, seventh, tenth or fifteenth med consumed that week. Choose to become less of a walking pharmacy by eating right, thinking positively, meditating and praying affirmatively, and exercising more.

- ☯ Wealth that's created for the benefit and health of people, and for the least harm to people and the planet is part of the circle of prosperity.

- ☯ Keep in mind that, from a MetaSpiritual perspective, previous errant thoughts, concepts, and beliefs that have laid the groundwork for your current woes are your own self-imposed 'ancestral wounds.'

- ☯ We have the pharmacy of pharmacies built into our DNA.

- ☯ *Cell*-ebrate your incredible cell power. Experience the awesome wholeness that comes from the reciprocity between 'Self to Cell' and 'Cell to Self' interconnectedness.

Know that mediocre selfcare is a meteoric route to illness and dis-ease.

- ☯ Don't dance competitively *just* to get to the winner's circle, play sports *just* to win, or compete in performing arts *just* for the acclaim and monetary recognition. Those are just 10% of the dividends. Let joy, passion, soul-deepening, and Self-Realization be 90% of the trip.

- ☯ We invite you to turn heeling into healing every chance you get. That is, turn heeling (accepting illness) into healing (seeing your body, mind and spirit whole and well.

- Lightening your karmic and emotional load is a form of 'weight training.'

- Our physical bodies are more verbs than nouns. By that we mean our bodies are dynamic living organisms that change each-consecutive-moment-of-now. Our cellular architecture, mental functioning, and emotionality are operating 24-7-365.

- Both mindful eating and mindless unhealthy eating are ways to become acquainted with the guidance of your inner nutritionists and pharmacists. Be wise enough to choose the better route.

- From cell to soul and soul to cell, your cellular body is a highly-charged sacred ground of Pure Energetic Beingness.

- Studies about mindless eating and obesity tell us that mindless eating actually distracts us from the act of eating itself, making us less sensitive to the body's cues of over-eating. This, in turn, prompts us to continue eating. Try a mindful eating meditation to switch this habit.

- Use the concept of firewalls! In the IT world, firewalls limit the data that can pass through them and protect a networked server from damage by unauthorized users. Firewalls typically establish a secure cyber  barrier between a trusted and secure internal network and another outside network, such as the Internet, is assumed to be unsecured. The term 'firewall' originally referred to a wall intended to confine a fire or potential fire within a building. Later, the term 'firewall' referred to structures, such as the metal sheet separating the engine compartment of a vehicle or aircraft from the passenger compartment. Using firewalls as a metaphor, we've coined the expression **'spiritual firewalls'** (denial statements that negate the illusionary power of outer appearances). In higher thought language, forging firewalls through the use of powerful denial statements helps you ward off the negative effects of false assumptions, biases, and impressions caused by mindlessly believing what you see and hear. So, deny the illusionary power of negatively-charged outer appearances to compromise your over-all health.

- When your "self" becomes consciously one with your "Self" you'll have achieved the epitome of selfcare, Selfcare, and Soulcare.

- The rise of alternative medicine and integrative medicine is changing the way the medical community practices medicine. If alternative medicine is placebic, give us more alternative cures. And there's one thing the medical community has always known about placebos – they work!

Be well aware that well-applied make-up and carefully-selected clothing may hide your level of fitness from others, but you can't fool a steep hill or a flight of stairs.

- Notice that it's important to practice moderation in moderation.

- Know that 96% of all chronic diseases are caused by a combination of poor food choices, toxic food ingredients, nutritional deficiencies, lack of proper physical exercise, lack of sleep, and over-consumption.

- Sugary drinks, like sugary praise, are among the most fattening things you can put in your body, mind, and soul.

- When you compromise your mental, physical, emotional, and spiritual health, you dampen your ability to consciously become one with your I-Am-ness.

- Be assured that when your soul is lifted up on the wings of positive, life-affirming thoughts, your body can be readily healed at both its subatomic level and cellular level.

- Suppose bacteria, metaphorically speaking, are invasive error thoughts and feelings that can become viral and weaken our sense of well-being? Also, what if bacterial infections suggest our over-all health being undermined by our own negativity?

- Physical *well*th is *cell*-ebrating your wellness biochemically, neurochemically, and emotively.

- Epigeneticists tell us that our positive and spiritually-oriented thoughts upregulate our genes and lead to our overall health and wellness.

- Affirm as often as you can: *"Because I'm the individualized Life Force of my Global Omnipresent Divine Nature actualizing Itself as me in human form, I lovingly declare all of the cells, molecules, and atoms in my body to be healthy, happy, and harmonious."*

- Don't brush your teeth immediately after meals which contain acidic foods and drinks (tomatoes, regular and diet sodas, citrus fruits, and sports drinks). These foods and drinks can soften tooth enamel 'like wet sandstone.' Brushing your teeth immediately after meals including these items can speed up the acid's effect on your enamel and erode the layer underneath. So, rinse well and then wait 20 to 30 minutes before brushing.

- The more you go into the Silence, the more you'll live out loud – *well*thily and wealthily as you gain more and more Y☯Univer**s**al Prosperity.

- Kudzu is an insidious vine that can absolutely take over an area. In fact, it's been nicknamed the "foot-a-night vine," the "mile-a-minute vine," and "the vine that ate the South!" Error thoughts can do the same thing to us! They start out small, but they can quickly dominate our thinking. Grudges, resentments and hurts – if we let them have space – will soon clutter our mental and emotional landscapes! We call these mental intrusions 'mental kudzu.' Pull it out by the roots!

Prefer prevention over intervention and intervention over neglect.

- Don't over-use antibiotics. Recognize that some of our best 'bio BFFs' are over 100 trillion 'good' germs that constitute what scientists call our microbiome. These microbes protect us from illness. However, our overuse of antibiotics and consumption of animal protein kill these useful microbes as well as the harmful ones. Almost 80% of the antibiotics sold are fed to livestock to beef them up so they can be slaughtered for higher profits. This causes drug-resistant bacteria to remain on meat and spread to us humans, resulting in antibiotic-resistant bacteria. Your well-being is based on a healthy body as well as a healthy mind and a healthy diet.

- Recognize that chemicalization is a sort of *spiritual floss*. It loosens the crust of old tapes, conventional assumptions, and subconscious thought patterns and helps you clean up your skin school acts.

- To achieve the Y☯Universal Prosperity you seek, be less dependent on your 'subconscious stream of consciousness' (Dead Sea), be more dependent on your enlightened waking consciousness, and be intentional in raising your heightened awareness to a Superconscious level (Upper Room). When you cross that higher consciousness threshold, you'll have negated the egocentric thought environment that infringes upon your *well*th and prefers the 'murky waters' of a materialistic and over-consumptive egocentric nature.

- Familiarize yourself with Qigong, which means 'life energy cultivation.' Qigong is the practice of aligning your body, breath, and mind for health, meditation, and martial arts training by balancing *qi* (Chinese for life energy which also includes heat, light, and electromagnetic energy) and achieving *gong* which is often translated as cultivation of work and skill mastery.

- Neuroscientists tell us that most of our decisions, actions, emotions, and behavior depend on the 95% of brain activity that's beyond our conscious awareness, which means that 95% of our thinking and behavior is influenced by the composite programming in our subconscious mind. The operative word is 'influenced' and not predestined! So, we must fill our current subconscious warehouse with positive, life-affirming thoughts and change the nature of our quantum (earth experience) programming.

- The wattage of your interior kundalini fire depends on the amperage of your spiritual practice.

- Keep in mind that previous errant thoughts, concepts, and beliefs that have laid some of the groundwork for your current woes are your own self-imposed 'ancestral wounds.'

- Karma isn't necessarily the evidence of fate, but simply the results of cause and effect. It's *kudzu* to the uninitiated, and a matter of choice to the wise who know they can re-cause their experience and avoid the negative effects of karmic hangovers from incarnation to incarnation.

> *Your physical body is your biological address. It's the 'somatic spacesuit' you lease to house your particular version of Spirit.*

- Cooking foods (above 165 F) destroys most harmful bacteria and other pathogens. If you eat uncooked foods like fruits or vegetables, they should be thoroughly washed with running treated (safe to drink) tap water right before eating.

- Understand that your errant thoughts, words, choices, and actions have a cumulative effect on your bodily systems and cellular ecology as long as you maintain a senseless attachment to divinity-denying habits and propensities. Work with your cellular community. Take care of your flesh and blood somatic container. Encourage it. Compliment it. Show it how much you care. Praise it. Thank it.

- Know that immunobiological research tells us we inherit more than just our genes from our parents. We also inherit epigenetic mechanisms for heart trouble, cancer, diabetes, and autoimmune disorders, etc. And, we also inherit important gene regulation propensities from our subconscious material which know how to harness the hidden disease-fighting wisdom in our genes.

- Because your connection to the Field of Infinite Potential is in your DNA, you can draw from the Field to attract and enjoy health and well-being by right of consciousness.

- When you harbor bitterness, resentment, anger and unforgiveness – your we*ll*th, happiness, peace of mind, compassion, and loving kindness will dock elsewhere.

- Practice medicinal spirituality so you can adopt a more enlightened perspective that cures any addictions to dogma, materialism and religiosity which retail fear, guilt and shame.

- Stay handcuff-free. Freeing yourself from egocentric defense mechanisms (handcuffs) allows you to keep a more positive outlook and view the world from an optimistic perspective. Taking handcuffs off liberates you from keeping yourself incarcerated in stale perspectives and self-defeating habits that can seriously interfere with your Y☯Universal health and well-being.

- Recognize that when you use positive, life-enriching affirmations, you alter the neural-circuitry that registers how you behave and what you believe. Each time you affirm your "I-Am-ness" with what we call the Global Omnipresent Divinity (G.O.D.), you strengthen your Y☯Universal connections.

- Here's the rub: whether you shower or take a bubble bath, you can improve your circulation and help your lymph glands drain by the way you towel off. We're not rubbing you the wrong way, are we? Seriously. Helping your lymph glands function can help prevent them becoming infected. And here's how. When drying off your limbs and torso, towel towards your groin area on your legs and towards your armpits on your upper body.

☯ Know that anomalous experiences like *déjà vu*, mystical visions, telepathy, stigmata occurrences, astral projection episodes, psychoneuroimmunological (spontaneous recovery and elevated immune system) responses, placebo effects, etc., that send you into a state of awe, astonishment, wonder, and even stupefaction are times when you experience *healthy* Y☯Universal chemicalization.

> *MetaSpiritually speaking, dandruff is the fall-out from error thinking and poor choices.*

☯ Drink more clean water. Stay properly hydrated. You need water to carry out body healthy functions, remove wastes, and carry nutrients and oxygen around your body. Six to eight glasses daily is sufficient. Drink at least a half glass of water before you continue this Health Matters section. Yes, right now! We'll wait!

☯ Realize that each cell, every molecule, each atom is a sacred tabernacle of Spirit. These sacred tabernacles are connected. There's no denominational sparring. Their biology is their collective theology. When we realize the significance of this invisible connection, we'll honor our relationship to our Divine Nature. When we acknowledge this connection, from soul to cell, our body becomes the highly-charged sacred ground of our being. When we achieve this perfect synchrony, we experience the *well*ness, joy, health, and wholeness which are the truth of our Y☯Universal Self.

☯ True *well*th is living at the speed of your Y☯Universal Extraordinary Self, which is your Soul Signature.

- You'll discover that the Bodhi Tree or Bo Tree, which is Sanskrit for 'awakening,' mentioned in the Eastern esoteric literature is a metaphor for your central and peripheral nervous systems (foliage), with the spinal cord (trunk) as the narrow sacred path to your spiritual awakening. And you'll gain other enriching insights from powerful MetaSpiritual, allegorical, and metaphorical literature that'll be the result of your evolving Y☯Universal Prosperity.

- Fast from negative thinking and poor eating habits.

- Your body is the psycho-somatic garment you wear during your matriculation through skin school. While it's not who you are, you need to take care of it – not mindlessly rent the garment, as they say. Except for a few alterations from time-to-time, it's the only 'quantum clothing' you'll have during your earth visit.

- Avoid using antibacterial soaps in bottles. There's no evidence that antibacterial soaps are more effective than regular ones. What's more, long-term exposure to some ingredients in these products, such as triclosan, may pose health risks.

- If scores of reincarnations have taught us anything at all, they've taught us that the point of power for actualizing our health and well-being is each-consecutive-moment-of-now regardless of what physical dimension we've chosen to matriculate through.

- Ethical veganism and vegetarianism are profound revolutions in our diet that reject centuries old paradigms of oppression and violence that have been programmed into the human race. These two higher consciousness dietary preferences are active commitments to eliminate any and all forms of irreverence, exploitation, violence and inhumanness toward animals, plants and ourselves.

- Understand that once you release them, the divine currents (*Qi, Vijñāna, Prana, Jivatma, Ki, Ch'i*, etc.) that run through your entire body will orchestrate your psycho-somatic *well*th and wholeness.

> Errant thoughts, choices, words, and actions are pixelations and should not be part of your soul growth diet. Avoid these pixelations so you don't get a distorted view of what your over-all health should be.

- Send white light and/or colored light to someone who isn't in close proximity to you. Pick a color that's related to the chakra that's associated with the area of the injury or illness. See the person surrounded with light. See any physical signs of his/her health issues dissolving and his/her body strengthening.

- Avoid second-hand smoke (breathing in air from smokers). It causes many of the same long-term diseases as smokers contract. According to the CDC (Centers for Disease Control and Prevention), there's no risk-free level of exposure to passive smoking! Please read that last sentence again. Even brief exposure can be harmful to your health. The bottom line – stay away from smokers while they're smoking and avoid cigarette smoke whenever you can.

- Avoid eating a large meal before sleeping, so you can decrease gastroesophageal reflux and weight gain. Also, avoid heavy meals in the summer months, especially during very hot days.

- Consciousness researchers who study 'psychological shielding' reveal that we can mentally block or even prevent any outside influences we don't want to influence us. We thought of the 'white light' technique we've been using for over 44 years. Some of you may use it. It's the one where you mentally surround yourself with a cocoon of energetic white light to protect yourself from harm, from things like someone else's cold, or cough, or illness, or injury, or negative thinking. It's a wonderful *well*th strategy.

- Consume a wide variety of different-colored fruits and vegetables. Why? Because fruits and vegetables with different colors represent different anti-oxidant content, which removes free radicals that damage your cells and fights inflammation in your body. Also, when you consume a large diversity of fruits and vegetables, it creates a wide variety of good bacteria in your gut, which creates a strong defense line between you and the environment, improves your immune system, and strengthens your long-term health. Even if you're a carnivore, veg out as much as you can.

- Avoid deep-fried foods. They contain acrylamide, a potentially cancer-causing chemical. Avidly avoid deep-fried foods. Did we say avoid *deep-fried foods*?

- You realize, of course, that the cumulative effect of poor dietary choices takes its toll. Isn't it a shame that too many people spend the first half of their lives learning habits that shorten the second half? Research tells us we are what we eat. In that case, nutty choices may be a staple in most people's diets. People have got to be a little nuts to eat what they eat sometimes. Despite compelling evidence that attests to the unhealthy side effects caused by fried foods, salt, white flour, sugar and alcohol, most people continue to ingest food products filled with them. One of the chief by-products of unhealthy food consumption is dis-ease.

- Our daily environments are filled with ringing phones, alarms of one type or another, the incessant chatter on TV's and radios, sirens, horns, the sound of traffic – all of which hijack our attention and keep us preoccupied with the pulse of the city. By contrast, natural environments gift us with the gentleness of their landscapes, the serenity which envelopes us as we wander down a tree hewn path, or see the valley below from a mountaintop. Taking a break from technological environments and stepping into the cocoon of nature is revitalizing and refreshing. It's blissful to be nurtured by Gaia's embrace. Echopsychologists remind us that our deepest roots are in nature. And it's within that deep rootedness with Mother Nature that we can find solace and connectedness.

- If they're functioning at a healthy psychosomatic level the vivified 'crown of thorns' (our spiritualized twelve pair of cranial nerves) will be energized by our fully opened Crown Chakra which will signal our complete Self-Realization. We'll have become consciously one with our Homo Deus Nature, having achieved the sought for perfection of our cosmic nobility.

- Try Alternative Nostril Breathing as a spiritual practice to insure better over-all health. Alternate Nostril Breathing (*Nadi Shodhana*) is a highly relaxing breathing technique that connects you with that deeper interior part of you. It releases accumulated tension and fatigue, centers you, and helps the brain hemispheres 'talk' to each other. As a spiritual practice it clears out and cleans blocked energy channels in the body, which integrates your body, mind, and soul connection.

- In social media terms, friendscaping refers to the act of 'trimming' your friends lists down to a reasonable number. From a Y☯Universal Prosperity, friendscaping means eliminating old habits and beliefs (old uninspiring and self-defeating 'friends') that used to define your old materialistic and fundamental religious pursuits in favor of new habits and beliefs that are more in line with your spiritual growth. Rather than focusing on 'breaking' old habits, put your energy into cultivating new habits and spiritual practices that are beneficial and nourishing. This healthy shift in mindset will allow you to focus on positive change by staying committed to the life you want, rather than focusing on getting rid of something you want to friendscape.

- When it comes to listening and/or reading about news coverage, lighten your 'news cycle load' by consuming good heart-centered news as well.

- Dine on MetaSpiritual Hors d' Oeuvres. They are metaphysical teachings. They also complement many basic theosophical, anthroposophical, allegorical, and metaphorical principles. A metaphysical interpretation of ANYTHING means seeing people, places, things, and events that happen 'out there' as human and spiritual qualities, talents, and abilities – as well as faults – within you. Read, study, absorb, examine, inquire, investigate, survey, research, and apply all of the MetaSpiritual knowledge you can as you question conventional unquestioned answers.

- Masterful meddling, as a Y☯Universal Prosperity practice, means knowing that *fact-facing* is just as important as *fact-finding* when it comes to expanding your spiritual perspectives. It implies understanding that wishbones and backbones are two different things. It means realizing you want to hold onto the right end of half-truths as you discover hidden truths.

- Try a form of Taoist yoga called Tao yin. It's characterized by a series of exercises that involve lying, sitting and standing positions. It's practiced by Taoists to cultivate ch'i, the internal energy (Life Force) of the body. The main goal of Tao yin is to create balance between your internal and external energies and to revitalize your body, mind and spirit.

- Be a 'trier of facts.' That means knowing that fact-*facing* is just as important as fact-*finding* when it comes to expanding your spiritual perspectives. The journey toward 'facts' can be fussy. It's usually fraught with unfounded assumptions, fossilized beliefs, cultural interpretations, disputed claims, unyielding biases, manipulative intentions, innocent misunderstandings, and fictitious assertions. Weaving through all of that muddy terrain can be frustrating. It'll take mettle – masterful mettle.

- *Yeukish inebriation* is an enthusiastic itchiness to explore higher truths (food for thought) once you've been intrigued by the depth of knowledge you're being exposed to. *Yeuk* is a middle English word for 'itch.' So, the next line of thought you find that excites your intellectual tastes and thirst for knowledge is the 'itch' we invite you to scratch! You'll naturally want more of it, a bigger taste. Your *yeukishness* will truly become a 'natural drug' that exponentially stretches your growing spiritual edge. Therefore, we enthusiastically give you the green light to explore your 'higher, more esoteric, thought itches.'

- Connect with your body's 'carrier waves.' This Y☯Universal Prosperity practice is based on some extraordinary findings in evolutionary biology. Evolutionary biologists suggest that all parts of our body know what's happening to all other parts via 'carrier waves.' This implies that our body's systems and organs are entangled which is a concept in quantum physics.

When you think about it, this entanglement is critical to the functioning of a biosystem as complex as our human organism. So, aligning your conscious intentions with your body's cellular consciousness can facilitate high speed healing. Talk to your cellular community. You can literally help orchestrate positive and life-affirming epigenetic responses to illnesses by adding your willpower to your body's evolutionary willpower to heal itself.

- Walking the spiritual path on practical, positive and prosperous feet is an exercise in 'spiritual podiatry.' MetaSpiritually speaking, feet stand for spiritual understanding. So, increase your over-all understanding of spiritual truths, principles, laws and teachings.

- Abstain from medical hexing. Medical hexing, from a medical standpoint, is the practice of a medical authority pronouncing a death sentence because it's believed that a patient has a 'chronic,' 'incurable,' or 'terminal' illness. However, from a MetaSpiritual point of view, medical hexing refers to any diagnosis or practice seen as assuming too rigid of a medical boundary. They're the ego's medieval walled city, erected out of limitation and maintenanced by fear. From an integrative medicine point of view – and from a spiritual perspective – there are no incurable diseases! Spontaneous remissions are commonplace in many health challenges, and are more commonplace than generally assumed. As a matter of fact, studies have shown that cases of spontaneous remission that aren't reported outnumber those reported by at least 10 to 1. We can tell you that the deeper roots of illness are unmapped by science. At the core of their healing, people who remised from their illness said they learned to let go of negative voices of criticism and self-criticism, and to see themselves as whole and complete. They talked to their cells, genes, organs and major body systems. They praised their cells and told their bodies how proud they were of the body's disease-fighting power. And here's the really telling finding: Many times it's the *belief* about a particular injury, disease, or accident type that 'kills' the patient – not the health challenge itself! Isn't that amazing!

> One of the most important things in life is the need not to accept downside predictions from experts.
>
> No one knows enough to make a pronouncement of doom.
>
> (Norman Cousins)

- ☯ We shouldn't discount the troubling news that's covered in the latest news cycle, nor should we simply disregard it if there's something we can do to make a difference. However, we also need to recognize what is and isn't under our control. Sooo, we invite you to remind yourself of that by staying objective – and sane – so you can work on what's within your power, interest and control. One thing you can do immediately is to affirm a more sane world - one that values compassion, loving kindness and enduring peace.

- ☯ Snack on 'sugar snacks.' A 'sugar snack' is a highly enjoyable, euphoric, and blissful spiritual concept that sends you to the heights of esoteric rapture. These 'spiritual snacks' are calorie-free spiritual wisdom, Theosophist theories, MetaSpiritual teachings and philosophical concepts that turn out to be delicious brain candy.

- When you like your work – and especially if you love what you do – you tend to perform well and are productive. However, when you're sick and absent from work (whether you're too sick to work or too dissatisfied to want to work), or remain at work, but fail to perform well, a copping out phenomenon called presenteeism occurs. Presenteeism means the entire performance of the organization suffers – people are present at work, but the presence of the quality and quantity of work actually performed is absent. That kind of disengagement isn't healthy for you or your workplace.

- Don't underestimate the 'night shift' (a good night's sleep). When our energy and well-being reserves are depleted and everything seems maddening, a good night's sleep (6 to 8 hours) recharges our well-being, energy levels, and sense of contentment.

- No matter how open, transparent, and loving they are, your relationships can break down at some point. There'll be conflicts and hard feelings occasionally. You can cushion the hard landings of human infallibility by showing undying respect for one another and holding each other in high esteem. Otherwise, cracks will appear in the edifice of a once thriving and *wellthy* relationship.

- Unfollow unprincipled, angry, fearmongering Twitter users who may fuel your own rage, and find unbiased and reputable news sources so you can moderate your own biases and broaden your perspectives.

- Turn dark data into smart data. In IT terms dark data is operational data that's not being used. In Y☯Universal Prosperity terms, your subconscious mind (dark data base) stores all of your previous life experiences, your cognitions, your beliefs and memories, all of the images you've ever seen, every thought and emotion you've ever had, all of your inclinations and intentions, and so on. It's the repository of your dreams, and, in our opinion, it includes the 'dark data' of your previous lives and reincarnational experiences. So, speak to it, and we mean actually speak out loud to your subconscious mind, compliment it for retaining the positive information it stores and encourage it to dispose of any and all information that can contribute to 'identity theft.' By that we mean train your subconsciousness to retain only the information that reinforces your True Spiritual Identity as a spiritual being having a human experience. Your subconscious will follow your lead and attract to you events and circumstances that reinforce your Authentic Divine Nature.

- ☯ Y☯Universal Prosperity IS the Breakfast of Champions!

- ☯ Some couples hesitate to give each other freedom and independence. This comes from a lack of trust and/or insecurity that if we give our partner too much space, he/she may discover they don't want to be with us anymore. Healthy couples make 'room' for one another's individuality and personal space.

- ☯ Don't narcotize yourself with doubt, fear, shame, guilt, or low self-esteem.

- ☯ Sitting is the new smoking! For people who sit most of the day, their risk of heart attack, stroke, cancer and diabetes is more dangerous than the health challenges associated with smoking. People are actually sitting themselves to death!

Plants need to be repotted periodically, to allow more room to grow and to replenish the soil with nutrients. If they are not repotted, the plants will become root-bound and unable to absorb sufficient water or nutrients to survive. Every once in a while, *repot* yourself with cutting edge spiritual perspectives and scientific findings so you don't grow "rut" bound!

- Take the advice of the Centers for Disease Control and Prevention. Calculate your heart rate for moderate-intensity physical activity by subtracting your age from 220. Then calculate 50-70% of that value. This percentage defines what your heart rate range should be. For example, if you're 20 years old, it should be between 100 and 140. If you're 70, it should be between 75 and 105.

- Understand that each person in your relationships has a subjective experience of what you experience as a couple, family, friends, etc. Acknowledge the differing perceptions and impressions of all of those involved. Work out any differences and biases as amicably, lovingly and respectfully as possible.

- Where your relationships are now is the cumulative effect of your past relationship's mutual choices, habits and shared outcomes – as well as your current relationships' mutual choices, habits and shared outcomes. Mindfully retool your relationships – as well as yourself – to arrive at healthier relationship outcomes.

- If your job requires you to engage with the news, here are several ways to unplug every hour so you can set boundaries related to your fast-paced news cycle responsibilities. Your health depends on it. Here is our 5-4-3-2-1 recommendation:

    ❖ Meditate for 5 minutes
    ❖ Look for 4 things around you that represent calmness and rest
    ❖ Find 3 things to listen to that represent happiness and joy
    ❖ Take 2 sips of coffee, tea or soda
    ❖ Touch your heart so you can feel it beating slowly and healthily

- Consider your own beliefs and biases, so you can choose to modify, release or even replace the ones that may compromise your *authentegrity* and/or negatively affect your relationships.

- Get a handle on your disappointments and anger. Uttering the wrong thing at the wrong time can steer your relationship in the wrong direction.

- Whether you hear the news on your way to and from work, read about it over breakfast, see it constantly regurgitated and analyzed repeatedly via online news outlets and TV programming platforms, it seems inescapable and particularly intrusive at times. And like it or not – or even being aware of its health implications – its sensationalized and repetitive negativity infuses itself into our psyche, taking direct aim at our over-all health and well-being. Recognize that optimism, an enlightened outlook, seeing light in the midst of darkness, affirming positive outcomes, and divinely ordering your own resilience are the emotional firewalls you need to protect yourself from negatively-charged news cycle content.

Selfcare is as important as the very air you breathe!

- Studies show that work – generally speaking – is good for your over-all health and well-being and that worklessness (is that a word) is associated with poorer physical, mental and emotional health.

- Avoid listening, watching, reading and discussing world news events a couple hours before bedtime. You risk having an anxious and sleep-deprived night.

- A lot of changes will take place when you're with someone for decades. And that'll mean loving each other through 'thick and thin' so your relationship continues to survive and thrive. And we're not talking about the 'small' stuff! Heavy stuff happens, things like: changes in religious beliefs and/or religions, becoming more spiritual than religious, serious life-changing injury, death of a family member (including children), end of life care for elderly family members, relocation, job loss, serious debilitating addiction, gender identification, sexual orientation, etc. The long term health of your relationship depends on your mutual adaptability, love and respect for one another.

- Listen to breaking news, but then delay your news consumption about the breaking news segment until more facts are aired. Watching or reading about breaking news reports gives us half-truths at best and plenty of speculation which serve to increase our anxiety and stress levels. Better to be Zen about it – go slow to go fast!

- Eliminate as many processed foods as you can. These foods cause imbalances in your microbiome and affect collagen bacteria (good bacteria) that keep your body healthy. Collectively your bacteria are known as 'gut microbiota,' and they protect against intestinal infections, produce vitamin K, and raise your immunity against diseases like arthritis, heart disease, and cancer.

- The Bible verse "Give us this day our daily bread" is a mistranslation, because the Greek word *epiousion* doesn't mean 'daily,' but supersubstantial, and *psomí* which means 'bread' is used instead of *hupostasis* which means spiritual assurance or sustenance. So, 'daily bread' really means 'uninterrupted assurance of Universal Substance.'

- Have you ever had what we call 'blessing fallout?' If you've ever said things like or agree with someone else saying things like *"the cancer blessed me,"* or *"lime disease blessed me,"* or *"a broken nose blessed me,"* or *"this heart attack was the best thing that ever happened to me,"* or *"getting fired blessed me,"* we call those frames of reference 'blessing fallout.' You're giving your power away and assigning a blessing on something that doesn't deserve to be blessed! Consider that what blessed you wasn't what happened to you, but *how you responded to what happened to you.*

- We recommend the following calorie-free spiritual opiums: compelling and transformative truth principles and riveting spiritual teachings; an out-of-body experience; beautiful music beautifully played and/or sung; a spiritual truth realized for the first time – and the second time, and the twentieth time, and the thousandth time; loving touch; a mystical experience; a child's laughter; an illness-free diagnosis; runner's high; a riveting meditational high and/or prayer experience; an astral travel experience; an encounter with an apparition; mental, emotional, and physical intimacy; a cathartic experience; a past lives regression experience; an 'ah ha' experience; a wonderful massage; etc.

- We refer to our physical body as a cosmic cube. Unfolding a cube turns it into a cross, which represents our human form with outstretched arms, forming a cross. Our carbon-based material form is the cross we bear.

- If you haven't picked up a good esoteric book lately for a buffet of higher consciousness reading, try binging on several of them for some spiritual sustenance. We call that going to a spiritual food court.

- Consider a cytonaut perspective when it comes to a deeper understanding of your cellular community. What that means is seeing human, animal, and plant cells as centers of spiritual and biological intelligence that can teach us how to appreciate the interconnectedness between cellular communities and our own health and well-being.
- Our bodies are temples of medicine. They provide cellular first responders, paramedics, pharmacists, anesthetists, allergists, respirologists, cardiologists, critical care practitioners, and emergency care specialists.

Spiritual Practice: Daily Affirmation for Health and Wholeness

I have now transcended all patterns and thoughts
of illness and pain.
I'm free and healthy!
My mind and body now manifest Divine perfection.
I love and accept my body completely!
I am good to my body, and my body is good to me.
I give thanks for ever-increasing health, beauty and vitality.
I am a radiant and vibrant actualization of
G.O.D. (Global Omnipresent Divinity)!

– Happiness Matters –

The Happiness Matters teachings we share are based on how well we experience joy, contentment, life satisfaction, and positive well-being, combined with a deep sense that our life is good, meaningful, and definitely worthwhile. It focuses on happiness with relationships, work, mental/physical health, communications, etc. – in other words, all aspects of your life! What's your Happiness Quotient?

Are you ready for some Happiness-related Y☯Universal Prosperity Hors d'oeuvres? Let's dig in!

- Google 'happiness' and you'll get over 3 billion hits (as of this writing). Giggle while you Google and you'll send oxytocin, dopamine and serotonin (the happiness hormones) to 37.2 trillion cells in your body. That's called Y☻Universal happiness because that's getting in touch with your Soul Signature' positive well-being.

- Research has shown that all of us have a kind of happiness baseline – that we seem to have a level of happiness that defines our general state of life satisfaction. However, using the tips (Rx's) we mention throughout this book, you can redefine your happiness baseline and enjoy a happier life. We promise. We wouldn't kid you about a thing like that. Your happiness quotient is too important.

- Wag more, bark less! And when you catch yourself losing it (barking more than wagging), say to yourself and/or say out loud, "Okay, calm down. I've got to wag more, and bark less."

- Schedule something you look forward to enjoying. It can be Facetime with a friend, a chocolate custard after lunch, or a walk in the park. Knowing you have this scheduled and taking just a moment to visualize doing it, releases dopamine in your brain *as if* you're actually doing it. In other words, you benefit from the visualized reward before actually getting the reward.

- Embrace positivity, and kick pessimism and negativity to the curb every chance you get.

- Understand that your moods and feelings are thought-driven, and can be changed in an instant by your next thought.

- Happiness is coming home from a hard day's work and being showered with love and affection by your faithful pet who's waiting at the door to greet you.

- Make sure you take time to make one or more of your 'signature strengths' a daily practice. For example, if you're really good at puns, or cracking jokes, or helping people feel loved and respected, or wordsmithing, or giving compliments, etc. – don't let a day go by without doing those things. They bring you joy and lift the spirits of other people who appreciate your vintage signature strengths.

- Find activities that you enjoy, ones that challenge you and increase your skill level at certain things. You'll more than likely find yourself happily engaged and immersed in what we call a satisfaction surge.

- Avoid being beside yourself, standing behind yourself, and getting ahead of yourself.

- Recognize that happiness is heart-to-head resuscitation.

- Realize that for every minute you're pessimistic you lose 60 seconds of happiness.

- Happiness, harmony, and joyfulness aren't condiments; they're three of the chief ingredients on your happiness resume.

- Don't sell 'negligible numbing' short. Negligible numbing is what happens when you catch yourself slipping back into an old habit, but notice it in time to prevent wholesale slippage. It's a particularly helpful practice when you find yourself using language that characterized your conversations when you were a product of the embedded theology that you've outgrown.

- Believe it or not, what you *think* about an event and how you respond to that event, are every bit as important as the actual event itself, and in some respects perhaps more important. See each event you experience as *in*formation. Let your *out*formation be joyful and happy.

- Turn frowns upside-down. Genuine smiles can trick your brain into happiness — and boost your health. A smile spurs a powerful chemical reaction in the brain that can help you feel happier. Psychologists have shown that the mere act of smiling can lift your mood, lower stress, and boost your immune system. Soooo, put on a happy face.

- Shoot a text or email, initiate a FaceTime or Zoom encounter, or go old-fashioned and write a letter to someone who makes you smile. Research shows those who foster connections tend to lead healthier, happier lives.

- Close your eyes and relive one of the happiest moments in your life! We're serious. Close your eyes and recollect one of your happiest moments before you read any further!

- Happiness is a Zenful nature. We can tell you – it's a Buddha-ful experience!

- Dial back your news consumption. Take a national news detox for a couple of news cycles or even a few days. Over-loading yourself with unpleasant, toxic and irritating news can sadden you, deplete your energy, and keep you angry and upset. Don't let a world that's gone bonkers do that to you.

- Happiness is listening to melodious gentle rain falling on a metal roof.

- Happiness is doing within while you're doing without.

- Opt for Holy Instants every day. They're happiness boosters! A Holy Instant is anytime you consciously calibrate (align, entrain, meld, fine tune, coalesce, fuse, amalgamate) your Human Nature with your Divine Nature.

- Neuropsychologists are telling us that neurons which fire together wire together. These 'wired' neurons not only create new neural structures, their 'firing together' can actually leave lasting impressions on our brains – even from fleeting thoughts and feelings. So, what we think and feel are critically important for our lasting happiness and wellbeing, and for our spiritual growth. We're not only the alchemists of our thoughts we're the alchemists of our neural real estate.

- See yourself as a source of happiness for others. You can't make others happy, of course, but your positivity and optimism will rub off on them and give them a faithlift.

- Dopamine, oxytocin, serotonin and endorphins are considered to be the brain's happiness chemicals. The first letters of each of those happiness chemicals, when combined, spell 'dose.' So, engineer a 'dose' of this happiness cocktail every chance you get. When you anticipate something good, dopamine is triggered. Oxytocin triggers empathy, trust, intimacy and sociability. Serotonin contributes to boosting your mood when you enjoy something and feel confident. Endorphins help you 'power through' challenges, pain and discomforts by looking for the silver lining.

- Find and 're-find' your True Self.

- Stay away from Same-o/Lame-o negative thinking which causes happiness drift.

- Listen to the tunes on your favorite playlist. Studies show that there's a strong link between listening to music you enjoy and feeling happy and content. Find comfortable seating and turn the volume control up, so you can 'bathe' audibly in the wonderful music you've chosen. The right content will help you feel content!

- Veto all notions of your own insignificance. You are an eternal spiritual being in temporary human clothing.

- Smile. Giggle. Laugh. Chuckle. Grin. Snicker. Clown around. Enjoy a PhD in happiness!

- If "you're happy and you know it, clap your hands," tap your feet, smile jubilantly, snap your fingers, jump for joy, laugh out loud!

- Be a "CAN-Guru" by bringing a positive spin to every conversation!

- Happiness is being in love with, and loved by, your soulmate and hearing "I love you" for the billionth time, and knowing that it's just as sincere as the first time you heard it.

- Drop the 'r' and turn your *r*elationship with happiness into an *e*lationship with happiness.

- Clarify your sense of purpose and meaning in life. Find those two qualities and you'll find lasting happiness. Think for a moment about the voice inside your head that's reacting to what you've just read. It's the Inner Compass you'll need to find the happiness you seek.

- Happiness goes against all of the principles of mathematics: it multiplies when its divided among people.

- People who say money can't buy happiness haven't shopped in the right places yet!

- If you trash talk yourself – stop it! It's blaspheming against your True Nature, which is divine.

- Do what you love, and if what you love provides you with substantial income to continue doing what you love, you're ahead of the game. Otherwise, be open to a variety of income streams that'll help support your doing what you love without having to worry about the finances involved in doing what you love.

- Why nostalgia hunting brings us unnecessary unhappiness: Trying to re-institutionalize nostalgic fantasies of the past by attempting to force-fit a future utopia to compensate for unrepeatable nostalgic remembrances usually sets us up for a series of heartbreaking disappointments and regrets.

- You are much more powerful than your thoughts. You have dominion over your thoughts. Thoughts are your creations by right of consciousness.

- Your brain operates like Velcro for negativity and Teflon for positivity. Train your brain to reverse that trend.

- What creates a sustained feeling of happiness, say experts, is a mixture of higher consciousness traits like optimism, positivity and resilience, fed by behaviors such as expressing gratitude, forgiveness and being kind to others - all held in sync by a strong sense of life purpose and oneness.

- Avoid the following four unhealthy relationship behaviors that can literally destroy happy relationships and lead to the end of your relationship. We're serious. Avoid these 'four horsemen of the relationship apocalypse.' Rein them in immediately:

    - Constantly criticizing your partner's looks, likes, character, and ideas. (Examples: "You look like something the cat drug in." – "You're so stupid." – "That's another one of your moronic ideas.")
    - Showing scornful contempt (constantly putting down your partner privately and in public, purposefully embarrassing your partner and making him/her feel worthless and inferior)
    - Habitually stonewalling (Example: withdrawing from an argument or disagreement intentionally by filibustering any attempt to work things out)
    - Blame-shifting (covering your own wrongdoing and intentional misconduct by placing the blame for your actions on your partner)

- Burst any and all 'filter bubbles' you may find yourself in. Filter bubbles are biased ideological frames of reference which are very slanted and don't provide a sufficient variety of opinions, thus, creating the impression that what they provide you is the only reality you need. Taking up residence in these highly opinionated bubbles won't give you the introspective bandwidth to achieve YⓊniversal happiness.

- Abracadabra-ing is using your seven Core Abilities (Authentegrity: a mash-up word combining Authenticity and Integrity), Intuitive Wisdom, Inner Strength, Questioning Unquestioned Answers, Optimistic Spirit, Self-Reliance, and Giving Consciousness), along with mindfulness meditation, affirmative prayer, visualization, open-mindedness, optimism, intuitiveness, mysticism, transcendentalness, metaphysical and esoteric teachings, and positive affirmations as the open sesames to happiness, healing, and enlightenment.

- Hugs, smiles, playful eye winks, compliments, kisses on the cheek, holding hands, rest, a soothing sip of hot coffee or tea, and mutual sharing of highly personal information are all forms of 'happiness acupuncture.'

Take a moment to list ten things that would trigger, or have triggered, your happiest moments. What would your 'decathlon of happiness' look like?

- The quality of your close relationships will keep you happier and healthier. Enjoying the closeness and security of warm relationships is therapeutic and protective. Period!

- A growing body of research strongly suggests that happiness improves your physical health; heightens feelings of positivity and fulfillment; improves cardiovascular health, elevates your immune system, reduces inflammation levels, and lowers blood pressure. Happiness has even been linked to a longer lifespan as well as a higher quality of life and well-being.

- Practice a little 'interior decorating.' YOUniversal Prosperity practice encourages adding higher, more spiritual thoughts and language, inclinations, knowledge, spiritual practices, etc., to your spiritual resume. It's based on cumulative knowledge and practice. It's an excellent practice to foster life-long learning and experiential exploration. As a spiritual practice it keeps you constantly engaged in higher thought and immersed in growing edge activities that deepen your appreciation for what it takes to be an enlightened being.

- Happiness brings a ray of sunshine to every square inch of us.

- Believe it or not, the shocking truth about prosperity is that it's not limited to a few. Each of us has the wherewithal to prosper. Religious accounts the world over are filled with rich promises about prosperity and abundance, especially when they're MetaSpiritually interpreted. They're YOUniversally-inspired prosperity textbooks for the ages.

- While it may be true that money doesn't buy lasting happiness, poverty doesn't either.

- Turn the pursuit of happiness into the happiness of pursuing your Greater Good.

- How many inconvenient truths might you be suppressing? An inconvenient truth is like trying to hold back a beach ball under water. Once you discover what's hidden, it's difficult to keep it hidden. And if the truth is compelling enough, you know it'll rise to the surface. And if it rises to the surface, it may upset your confirmation bias. However, let it rise you must. You'll be happier and more fulfilled knowing you've moved from fiction to fact, from fallacy to truth.

Simba, the lion cub in the Lion King saga, reminds us that *'Hakuna matata'* (no worries, worry-free living) is the best practice.

- Finding meaning in your life is one of the key predictors of how happy you'll be – and remain.
- Increase the attention you give to what is nourishing for you, to what sustains you, to what brings you happiness.
- Happiness is hearing children giggling as they play in the park and then getting the giggles yourself.
- Happiness is maintaining a proper mental and emotional *al*titude over your life experiences.
- If you continue to replay a thought that's negative and getting in the way of your happiness, literally toss it away. Write any toxic thoughts about yourself on a piece of paper or flash paper, then shred it or burn it. This 'burning bowl' or shredder practice has been shown to improve your feelings and help you feel a sense of accomplishment. It might sound a little ridiculous, but give it a try. You've got nothing to lose, but – well - your negativity and sadness!
- Happiness happens in each present moment. So, fill each consecutive-moment-of-now with positivity, optimism, faith lifts, cheerfulness, and joyfulness.
- Defriend any and all negative subconscious tendencies and self-defeating patterns that percolate up into your waking consciousness.
- Happiness is enjoying living in joy.
- Limit the energy you give to whatever saddens you.
- Happiness is enjoying and maintaining fully functioning Y☯Universal Prosperity in your life.
- Notice that your thoughts are the children of your Y☯Universal Consciousness, so give birth to loving, compassionate, joyful, kind, and spiritually-inclined children.

- In terms of your over-all happiness and contentment, make 'keystone species' a habit. From an ecological perspective, keystone species play critical roles in maintaining the structure of an ecological community relative to the keystone species biomass. For example, conservation biologists tell us that elephants are a 'keystone species.' Their role is analogous to the function of a keystone in an arch. Just as an arch will collapse without its keystone, any other species and even entire ecosystems would become extinct without a keystone species. Examples of keystone species are: sea stars, jaguars, grizzly bears, sea otters, prairie dogs, and beavers. Meditation, affirmative prayer, positive affirmations and resolute denials, visualization, MetaSpiritual interpretations of sacred texts, Self-Realization practices and forgiveness are "keystone species" that are necessary conditions for spiritual growth and development. Without these spiritual technologies, your spiritual practice may collapse. They're essential spiritual technologies.

- Not every issue, problem, or challenge has a happy solution; some issues, problems, and challenges just have to be survived so you can move on with dignity and grace. It's important to recognize that happiness isn't circumstantial, it's simply the omnipresent joyfulness that's built into your Y☯Universal Prosperity.

- Money can lessen the amount of unhappiness and concern about making ends meet, but it doesn't guarantee lasting happiness, according to the research. Money, per se, does buy freedom from worry about basic needs like – shelter, food, clothing, everyday expenses, transportation and emergencies.

- Turn 'post-traumatic stress' into 'post traumatic growth.' You'll be happy you did.

- Define what 'selfcare' means to you – then see it as a daily spiritual practice. The thing about small 's' selfcare (your human self), if you don't find time for taking care of yourself at that level of being, you'll probably neglect to take care of yourself at the capital 'S' Selfcare level (your higher consciousness Self-Realization level, your Divine Nature).

- Happiness is sleeping in on a given day and looking forward to a clockless day.

- Have you ever felt your lungs inflate with the onrush of a happy moment? It's called being 'happified!'

- Here's one way of looking at happiness: Let's say you're a happy person. If people want to be around you, they can either express their happiness too, choose to be happier than they were, or follow the signs to the nearest exit! Doesn't that make sense!

- Happiness is nirvana. Unhappiness is unnerved-vana.

- Money may not buy lasting happiness, but wouldn't you rather pout in a Mercedes, BMW or Bugatti La Voiture Noire than on a city transit bus.

- Purge all thoughts of lack and insufficiency from your consciousness.

- Divorce, defriend, withdraw from, disassociate yourself from, put an end to, terminate – any and all forms of unhappiness.

- Be unapologetically happy. Happiness is making the current *you* the best Y☯Universal version of yourself.

- Happiness is wading in a stream barefoot.

- Getting smart about your 'happiness quotient' means dumbing down your base instincts toward greed, selfishness and personal aggrandizements.

- Well-being is, well, being your True Self. It's the Extraordinary You, the YOU that's achieved Y☯Universal Prosperity. It's the happiness you achieve by the incredible 'happen-ness' you Divinely Order as a powerful spiritual being who has chosen a human experience.

- Everyone who isn't happy should be shot … up … with a *dose* of the happiness chemicals: dopamine, oxytocin, serotonin and endorphins.

- Research has found that people who favor 'experienced happiness' over 'remembered happiness' mostly expressed a belief in *carpe diem*: the philosophy that one should seize the present moment, because the future is uncertain and life is short. On the other hand, participants' explanations for choosing 'remembered happiness' over 'experienced happiness' expressed a desire for a longer lasting happiness which took the form of a nostalgic treasuring of happy memories. Interesting huh. By the way, which one do you prefer? Our preference is a hybrid approach. We value both our happy experiences AND our reminiscing about them; however, we also make it a practice to experience happy times as often as we can.

- Lasting happiness is gaining clarity between the House of Wanting, the House of Needing and the House of Having.

- Reject any form of envy, jealousy, or harsh criticism which dampens your self-esteem and *worth*ship.

- You can't build your current happiness on the 'unhappinesses' in your past. Begin today to fill your waking consciousness with happiness, which will program happiness into your subconscious reservoir and vaporize the unhappinesses that have taken up residence there for much too long.

- A 2017 study published in the *Proceedings of the National Academy of Sciences* showed that people who spent money on things that helped them save time – delivery or cleaning services, lawn services, for example – were more satisfied than if they bought more bling or expensive wine. Having more time to do the things they really enjoyed incentivized their making even more time to enjoy the things they found enjoyable.

- Dismiss any feelings of inferiority and unworthiness. Fast from all self-doubt, and concern about being worthy and good enough.

- No matter what you believe to the contrary – you can go from error to eros.

- Happiness is winding down on the back porch with a glass of wine or cup of coffee or tea after a long work day.

- One of the most powerful actions you can take for your spiritual growth is to take conscious control of the 'critters' trying to overtake your mind - critters like: fears, doubts, false beliefs and assumptions; negative thoughts and emotions - all the stuff that's debilitating and draining. They can overtake you as surely as those wildlife critters can take over your yard, basement or attic! BUT, you have the power to control them. All you have to do is stop feeding those self-negating critters!

- People who are bankrupt of joy or boycott happiness are missing many lifelong annuities of perpetual YOUniversal Prosperity.

- As it turns out, self-control and self-reliance learned in childhood are two of the best predictors of health, wealth, and happiness in adulthood.

- The past doesn't have to define you – or confine you. Smile your way to nirvana. Grin your way to Y☯Universal Prosperity.

- Happiness is finishing all of the laundry, buying groceries, getting my hair and nails done, and cleaning house – and still having a free weekend to look forward to.

- Happiness is an acquired taste. So, acquire it often in each and every one of your lifetimes to come.

- The unenlightened ego is a form of Adamic arsenic. It's poisonous to your over-all happiness and contentment.

- MetaSpiritually speaking, an 'adept' is a highly evolved spiritual idea, sacred spiritual principle, or divine insight. 'Adepts' are precursors to lasting happiness!

- Be careful of high a standard you set for happiness based on what the popular media touts. Setting high standards for your own happiness as a function of what media says is true – may be based on hype and not evidence. For example, you may think it's true that you should be happy all the time, or extremely happy on a daily basis. That can set you up to feel disappointed with yourself if you don't feel happy 24-7-365. You may believe you fall short on the happiness scale – and that could have detrimental effects on what you believe the true nature of happiness is. Here's what we believe: short term dissatisfaction and disappointments are perfectly normal. After all, we're in skin school and subject to occasional setbacks. Happiness isn't contingent on what happens to us. It depends on how much our response to what happens to us is based on the knowledge that, as spiritual beings who've chosen a human experience, we can divinely order any amount of happiness we want, anytime we want, for as long as we want!

- March 20th is the International Day of Happiness. However, it goes without saying – although we're going to say it anyway – *every day* can be seen and enjoyed as a day to experience happiness.

- Don't *do* dogma of any breed. Why? Because any attempt to give dogma even an iota of credence leads inevitably to emotional vertigo and unhappiness.

- Fuel each of your coming reincarnational and incarnational journeys with truckloads of happiness.

- Live and relive the happiest version of your True Self in whatever dimension of being in which you find yourself – oh, wait – that includes the current you!

- Know that the word *limitation* has the words *limit* and *imitation* in it. It doesn't take a giant leap in insight to see that whenever we repeat (*imitate*) self-defeating thoughts and behavior, we *limit* what we can be. We limit our happiness and joy whenever we repeat self-defeating subconscious patterns and tendencies.

- Happiness is hand-holding walks with your significant other.

- Before we can find happiness and peace in our current human incarnation, we've got to transform the negative patterns in our subconscious universe.

- The rider on a donkey theme in esoteric religious literature is a common MetaSpiritual symbol. The rider represents our Soul Signature status, our Higher Self, our Divine Nature, the Enlightened Us, the Extraordinary Us, our Authentic Self. The donkey symbolizes our lower self, the unquickened spiritual us, our egocentric human personality – characterized by its stubbornness, material addictions, divinity-denying mindset, and an unwillingness to surrender to our Y☯Universal Nature.

- Dismiss the old debilitating patterns, preferences and habits that insult your evolving Y☯Universalness.

- Upgrade your happiness from "Happiness is a state of mind" to 'Happiness is a state of mine!"

- Practice '*conscious satsang*.' Conscious *satsang* refers to filling your consciousness with thoughts, intentions and inclinations of higher spiritual truths to show your devotion to your spiritual growth. *Satsang* is a Sanskrit word that means 'gathering together for the truth.' Conscious *satsang* not only leads to enlightenment, it helps to ensure your happiness getting there!

- Whatever happiness people get from their worship of religious dogma will, unfortunately, limit the happiness they can derive from questioning the staleness of unquestioned religious answers.

- Awakened being, awakened doing, and awakened having constitute the mindfulness trinity that will set you free from the centrifugal force of mindless materialism and bring you the lasting happiness you seek.

- Marine Sgt. Jonny Joseph Jones lost both of his legs in an explosion while serving in Afghanistan. We were struck by a quote of his we saw recently. He said, "People ask how I stay so positive after losing my legs… I simply ask how they stay so negative when they have both of theirs."

- Neuroscientists are studying a gene variant that leads to higher levels of the brain chemical called anandamide, which contributes to our sense of calm, happiness, contentment and bliss. We wonder if there'll ever be a pill for instant happiness in humankind's future!

- You've probably heard the expressions, "He/she's only human" or "It's human nature." Those expressions are generally used to excuse mistakes and poor choices. And they're based on the notion of our unworthiness and sinfulness, two terms used by those still stuck in pediatric theology. The truth is, we're divine by nature. The mistakes we make don't come from our True Nature, they come from our lack of human nurture in our current and past skin school appearances. The mistakes we make come from the bruised, selfish, frightened, unenlightened egocentric patterns warehoused in our subconsciousness.

- Become a happy 'new YOU-ologist' where you are potted and repotted each day, born and reborn each day. We call this spiritually oriented 'new you process' *spiritual obstetrics*.

- Sense consciousness is unfortunately cosmetic consciousness. Its promiscuous affair with materialistic trappings is evidence of an unenlightened ego's attachment to human form (The Tree of the Knowledge of Good and Error). The sooner we prune ourselves from the worship of outer appearances the sooner we'll awaken from our sleep.

- If you're wearing a mask of fear, or guilt, or unworthiness, or anger, or jealousy, or worry, or envy, or revenge, or greed, or hatred, or unforgiveness, or anxiety, or pride, or any other kind of self-diminishing mask – it's time to move beyond your 'mask confusion.'

- Metaphysically, the symbolic act of 'foot washing' actually refers to the other end of our body – the intellect in our head! Washing means 'cleansing' and feet represent 'spiritual understanding.' So, when you cleanse (wash) your waking consciousness of error thoughts and inclinations you elevate your spiritual understanding (feet) so you can achieve the happiness you seek.

- Happiness is not sabotaging your next thought, choice or action with yesterday's poisonous patterns.

- Become addicted to *Self-Realization* (aligning yourself with your Divine Nature), to health and wholeness, to loving kindness and compassion, to unconditional love, to forgiveness, to fair play, to smiles and laughter, to hugs and handshakes, to Namaste-ing everyone, to *thanksliving*, to daily Sabbath experiences, to world peace, to an end to war and eliminating world hunger, to altruistic living, to MetaSpiritual scriptural interpretation, to affirmative prayer and meditation, to life-affirming spiritual practices, to humankind's collective welfare.

- Looking outside yourself for happiness is delusion trafficking. Your emotional *well*th is within.

- Create neocortex moments which foster neuroplasticity (adding new mental real estate). They'll keep you out of negativity and the myriad limitations championed by the amygdala, and move you toward the positivity and optimism you'll need for perpetuating your Y☯Universal Prosperity.

- Recognize that each life-affirming thought you have, word you speak, choice you make, and action you take is an altar to your evolving Y☯Universal adeptship, tranquility and happiness.

- Happiness is getting out of credit card debt.

- Get in the practice of Divinely Ordering your good (health, happiness, inner peace and sound money matters). Divinely Ordering your good is the conscious process of allowing your over-all *well*ness to flow *from you and through you*. It's affirming your Greater Good by right of consciousness. It's recognizing that the Infinite Field of Potential is available to you each-consecutive-moment-of-now!

- ☯ 'Feng Shui' your thinking so your thinking leads to right choices and actions. And that implies living from a spiritual perspective so your actions are consistent with your BS (belief system) and values that lead to lasting happiness.

- ☯ Re-language old religious concepts with MetaSpiritual terminology that reflects where you are spiritually. That's the kind of Tongue Fu that leads to creating Y☯Universal happiness and harmony.

- ☯ Do you want to live on the cutting-edge of enlightened thought or the dull-edge of stale conventional thinking?

- ☯ ***Know*** yourself before you ***no*** yourself. *Self-Realization* isn't an egotistical, superficial scheme to claim your uniqueness as a divine being. We're all rare, complicated, and all-too-delicate spiritual beings wrapped in our own particular somatic packages of DNA when we're in skin school. The speck of consciousness which becomes the human us bursts into personhood, remains for a time, then vanishes again as we soar to our next adventure in consciousness. So don't waste time looking outside yourself to find your Self.

- ☯ Prune thoughts of your unworthiness, over-consumptive appetites, chronic poor choices, self-destructive actions, and unquestioned religious beliefs from your consciousness, because they're the 'yeast of your unhappiness!' Will this guarantee that our great-great-grandchildren will live happy and satisfying lives? We'll see. However, our sense is that human nature is much more than biology.

- ☯ Every time you experience the acoustics of happiness it's because you've experienced the resonance of your alignment with your Divine Nature.

- Recognize that nothing can ever be taken from you that's yours by right of consciousness.

- Fasten your seat belt. Geneticists are developing nanoscale technologies that marry robotics and traditional pharmacology. These "mood bots," once ingested, will travel directly to specific areas of the brain, flip on genes, and manually turn up or down our happiness and mood set points. Welcome to 21st century happiness technology that can literally program our neurophysiology. Will it be a panacea or a Pandora's Box?

- Understand that when we give, it's truly an affirmation of our belief in abundance. Because when we think lack, we hold on to what we have; we hoard it; we protect it. But when we feel like we have a lot, we freely share it.

> Be willing to let go of your good for your GREATER good! Sometimes we get so caught up in what we have - because it's so good - that we blind ourselves to something even better! We keep ourselves in a half empty box, and get stuck there.

- Constantly remind yourself that prosperity isn't something that comes *to* us. It comes *through* us.

- Our good, *in potentia*, is a thought, an intention, a choice and an action away.

- Realize that lulls in prosperity are to be overcome, not for you to be overcome by their illusionary power.

- Many people have a hard time believing dancing is spiritual and that truly connects us to our inner core. Most people feel awkward and self-consciousness when it comes to dancing. Dance, as a legitimate spiritual practice, lets your movement come from the inside out. Dancing gives you an opportunity to express your goodness via joyful, blissful movement. It hints at the divine dance within us, the positive well-beingness that's in our DNA.

- Note that when we move out of a lack consciousness, a fear orientation, a guilt predisposition, an unforgiveness mode – and into a consciousness of abundance, we'll enjoy incredible *well*th and wealth.

- 'Absolively, positutely' understand that neither Wall Street nor government stimulus packages will determine your lasting prosperity, because they're not your Source. Downturns in the economy can't handcuff you because they're not, never have been, and never will be what determine or limit the good you can create by right of consciousness. Work toward and achieve YOUniversal Prosperity and you'll 'absolively, positutely' know that this declaration is true.

- Attachments are ornamental reactions to something we feel we need to complete us, to make us happy, to feel we're worthy. Felt abundance is the recognition that we're already whole at the level of Spirit.

- What you bless multiplies and grows. A blessing means 'to confer prosperity upon.' So, always bless, confer prosperity upon, what you want to manifest — and in so doing, you'll create an unending ripple effect of prosperity and abundance.

- We're convinced that one of the chief blocks to people manifesting their good is what we call Intention Deficit

Disorder, which is another word for unactualized intentions. It's the "taking action, rolling up our sleeves, and knowing without a doubt that we can divinely order our good intentionality" that brings us the results we want. And by the way, you've probably heard of the age old expression 'necessity is the mother of invention.' We've updated it to say 'necessity is the mother of *intention*.' It's intention acted upon that leads to inventions!

- If you catch yourself succumbing to iffy-ness (mental laziness), simply turn your *attention* back to your *intention* in order to manifest what you want.

- The most popular class in the history of Yale University, 'Psychology and the Good Life,' was inspired by a paradox. The psychology professor puts it this way: Even when people, conventionally speaking, succeed - get into a top tier college, make lots and lots of money, accumulate tremendous prestige and receive accolades from famous people - they're often left feeling unsatisfied and not as happy as they thought they'd be.

- Many people's happiness seems to be based on comparisons - in other words, on how what we have compares with what others have, not on whether what we have happens to be good for us. For example, some telling research at Yale looked at Olympic medalists:

- Those who won gold were visibly thrilled and pleased with themselves after their event. However, bronze medalists appeared happier on the medal stand than silver medalists. That's because, the Yale study postulates, each medalist's reference point was from a different perspective. The silver medalists were probably fixated on the gold medal they didn't get, but the bronze medalists were most likely thinking about the fact that they could have received no medal at all.

- What if the Holy Grail that the Grail legends talk about is the Y☯Universal Prosperity we talk about? When we fully align our Human Nature with our Divine Nature we can achieve the enlightenment and Self-Realization we need to enjoy Y☯Universal Prosperity in our current skin school experience.

- Share any good news with someone lately? Studies show that sharing good news can have a positive impact on our well-being and is instrumental in ensuring that we are happy and in good health.

- *Forelsket* is a Norwegian term that refers to the happiness and euphoria we experience when we first fall in love. Spiritually speaking, a *forelsket* reaction is the euphoria and bliss we feel when we first come across a compelling spiritual truth, see its implications for transforming our lives, and love how it expands our consciousness. Stay open to the transformational value of serendipitous spiritual teachings that redefine your growing edge.

- Take 365 vacations this year! Is that a great happiness benefit package or what? We're serious! Before you freak out, let's define what we mean by a vacation. A vacation is any specific amount of time in your day, from as little as 15 minutes all the way up to a full 24 hour day, where you intentionally choose to do some activity that's focused on your personal growth spiritual enrichment. It's a vacation that ups your vacation and enjoyment meter.

- Friendscape your way out of unhappiness. In social media terms, 'friendscaping' refers to the act of 'trimming' your friends lists down to a reasonable number. From a MetaSpiritual perspective, 'friendscaping' means eliminating old habits and beliefs (uninspiring and self-defeating friends) that used to define your old materialistic and worldly pursuits in favor of new habits and beliefs that are more in line with your spiritual growth.

- Make kookaburra hilarity a habit! This Y☯Universal Prosperity practice has an unusual name, but its relevance will become obvious in a few moments. It's about good-natured merriment and its name  comes from 'down under.' In Aboriginal Australian terms a kookaburra is a rather large bird that has sounds that echo hysterical human laughter. Are you laughing good-naturedly yet? Hysterically yet? You can add a happy dance if you want!

- Celebrate the acoustics of *thanks-living*. It's filled with the harmonics of thank you's. *Thanks-living* is a practice that makes peace with the past and adds humility to the present. *Thanks-living* places you above the ups and downs of everyday living. It's a life in which you aren't held captive by the centrifugal force of outer appearances. It's a life of perpetual gratitude, a life of being grateful for what you have.

- Happiness is working all things together for good. Notice we didn't say work most things, or some things, or almost all things, or a few things together for good. The Y☯Universal principle is: When you synergize your Human and Divine Natures, when you consistently make choices based on that Y☯Universal synergy, you'll be able to work **all** things together for good.

- Doubt and feelings of unworthiness are self-addressed 'happiness pitfalls' that will keep you from achieving the enduring happiness and contentment you seek.

- How many people do you know that are genuinely happy? We don't mean happy because they've just met the man or woman of their dreams, or because they've won the lottery, or have bought a new SUV, or a new house or beach house, or gotten a job promotion. We're talking about being deeply inwardly happy and content. We're describing a wellspring of inner serenity, life satisfaction and joy. How many people do you know like that?

- Form follows thought. Everything material (form) follows the thoughts that create it. Sooo, hold prosperous thoughts about your health, inner peace and financial security, and you'll create the realities you want in life.

- Live on the cutting edge of enlightened thought, not on the dull edge of dogmatic conformity. You'll find there's much more happiness and insightfulness at that level of heightened awareness.

- Enter each experience with a feeling of positivity and self-composure. Research from behavioral genetics has revealed that a full 50% of our happiness results from our intentional acts that bring us a sense of satisfaction and control.

- Cultivate interests with others who share your interests and values because, according to positive psychologists, it's one of the most important lifestyle factors that raises your over-all happiness quotient.

- Capitalize on the positivity of good days, and minimize the negativity of downer days.

- Ten thousand people from 47 different countries were asked what they valued most in life. Happiness received the top billing, beating out love, money, health and getting to heaven.

- Emotions like joy, contentment, life satisfaction, and cheerfulness broaden our brain hemispheric synchronization and enable us to expand the bandwidth of our thinking and problem-solving.
- Social comparisons - via social media platforms like Facebook, Instagram, WhatsApp, WeChat, Messenger, LinkedIn, etc. – can be thieves of personal happiness.

It's not how many good or distressing things that happen to us that determine how happy we are, but which things we focus on the most.

- The neurobiology of happiness suggests that the brain areas associated with sensory pleasures (food and drink, drugs, intimacy) overlap with those for higher-order pleasures (artistic, altruistic, transcendental experiences).
- Some people we know have reached the age where happy hour is a long nap!
- Avoid antidisestablishmentarianism antics. Why? Because it's our propensity for not wanting to withdraw the unenlightened ego's rulership over our human personality.
- Much of our unhappiness comes from tying ourselves up into 'knots of nots.' That means knots of: not being good enough, not having enough, not feeling prosperous enough, not letting go enough, not holding on long enough, not listening enough, not releasing anger enough, etc.

Spiritual Practice: Do It With Joy!

This activity is designed to increase your awareness of the fact that Heaven is a state of consciousness — one you can choose at any moment regardless of what is going on in the world around you.

Here's How:

As you find yourself facing some task you dread, or a situation that is stressful, pause and consciously choose joy.

You might adopt a mantra such as: **"Since I have to do this anyway, I choose to do it with JOY!"**

Notice the change it makes, not only on your own attitude, but on the situation itself. You will be surprised at how much easier and more productive things will be when you approach them from an attitude of joy.

– Inner Peace Matters –

The Inner Peace Matters teachings we share are based on how well we experience peace of mind, serenity, calmness, bliss, Inner Strength, and freedom from anxiety or stress. It describes a high state of consciousness, one where we have achieved enlightenment and Self-Realization through disciplined use of spiritual practices.

Are you ready for some Inner Peace-related Y☯Universal Prosperity Hors d'oeuvres? Let's dig in!

- Be willing to release any attachment you have to anger, resentment, regret, revenge, etc., for any hurtful thing someone has done to you – and what you may have done to yourself – so these negative emotions don't form outposts in your consciousness. That's the true nature of forgiveness and the inner peace that comes with it!*

- Be aware of any self-defeating copycat choices you're making. If you find yourself moving into a copycat routine, ask yourself: "Why am I choosing imitation over authenticity?"

- Don't major in minor things.

- Eliminate all forms of *inner paparazzi* (persistent regrets; reoccurring bad habits, choices and behaviors) which limit or block your attaining the inner peace you seek.

- An unenlightened ego says "Once everything falls into place, I'll feel the inner peace I seek." The Extraordinary Y☯U says "Find the inner peace within and everything else will fall into place."

- We recommend an "I" doctor for anyone neglecting to walk the spiritual path on happy, cheerful, optimistic, joyful, blissful feet.

- Recognize that since materialism is usually wrapped in horizontal consciousness, it'll always be vertically challenged.

- You've heard of 'peace of mind.' Why not refer to it as 'peace in mind' since that implies a peaceful intention!

- Have the courage to awaken the kundalini energies within you on your quest for the inner peace that comes from your Self-Realization journey. Make it a spiritual practice to 'tame your dragon' by vitalizing each of the seven main chakras so that their synchronization strengthens your Life Force from your Root Chakra to your Crown Chakra.

- Enlightenment is better than puzzlement, if only for spiritual reasons.

- Try a little vertical farming. That means seek highly advanced spiritual teachings (skyscrapers). In an agricultural context, vertical farming is the practice of cultivating crops in and on top of skyscrapers. The higher teachings we're prescribing are most likely considerably beyond your normal spiritual 'reads.' They're more esoteric and MetaSpiritual in nature.

- Diddlysquat order is the opposite of divinely ordering our experience. Actually, it's error ordering! It's the cause of abnormal fluctuations, disturbances, and disorder – which are all ghosts of our poor choices which cause outer war instead of inner peace.

- See Intuitive Wisdom which is centered in inner peace, as a cognitive firewall that protects you from irrational thinking, ridiculous choices and preposterous actions.

- The neuroplasticity of MetaSpiritual thought will rewire your spiritual perspectives and prune the dogma from your religious beliefs synapse by synapse.

- Step beyond Scarecrow-ology. Trust your relationship with the awesome Power within you called GOD (your Great I AM Presence, the Global Omnipresent Divinity, the Eternal Presence, the Infinite Isness, or whatever name you give to the Omnipresent Intelligence which is the Ground of All Being). Tap into your Inner Strength, inner peace, and resoluteness so you can meet any challenge or difficulty. It reminds you that changing the position of two letters (the 'c' and the 'a') in s*ca*red becomes s*ac*red. It means you don't have to cower to the scare tactics of a chaotic world. You have the wherewithal to meet any worldly challenge.

- Inner peace changes the crush of negative circumstances into the hush of positive, life-affirming circumstances.

- Prosperity doesn't have to play peekaboo with you. It can be sustained uninterrupted when you don't interrupt your peaceful, positive thoughts with negative ones.

- Remind yourself that worrying, fretting, and anger won't cancel tomorrow's troubles. They'll take away today's peace and serenity.

- Give up falsehood for the truth, defriend fiction for facts, and turn mileposts into smile-posts.

- Inner peace is an antidote to despondency and depression, and a neutralizer of worry and irritation.

- According to neuroscience, a peaceful state of mind increases gray matter (neuroplasticity); accelerates your thinking capacity; improves memory and attention; and expands the bandwidth of your ability to conceptualize and appreciate higher realities.

- Realize that the phrase "born again" is referring, in a very real sense, to a kind of *spiritual obstetrics* where we birth ourselves into a higher spiritual understanding which clarifies who and what we really are as Divine Beings in human 'clothing.'

- Detox yourself from toxic people – and you'll find inner peace. Declutter yourself from unhealthy relationship clutter – and you'll enjoy inner peace. Retire from tiring circumstances – and you'll unearth inner peace. Vacate unfulfilling work as soon it's reasonable – and you'll achieve inner peace. Forgive yourself and others for what needs to be forgiven – and you'll have inner peace.

- What you genuinely appreciate – usually appreciates sooner than you think. Sooo, appreciate inner peace which is the kind of peace 'that passes all misunderstanding.'

- Inner peace is unruffled composure and poise when we're under pressure from the noise of outer circumstances.

- You can find inner peace in a whirled world 'out there' by going within to the serenity 'in here' – we're pointing to your head-heart connection.

- Tranquility, blissfulness, nirvanic calmness, serene composure and self-assured steadiness are all ways to spell inner peace.

- Speak in tongues. Let's be clear here! We're not referring to the traditional religious practice of 'speaking in tongues.' From a MetaSpiritual perspective, the phrase 'speaking in tongues' symbolizes your ability to communicate deeper meanings of hidden truths. That  means sharing esoteric truths, metaphorical truths, mystical truths, cabalistic truths, theosophical truths, spiritual truths, and anthroposophical truths in such a way that people can understand and appreciate them. It's this interpretation of 'speaking in tongues' that defines this nuance of inner peace.

- Every now and Zen look inside yourself for the peace you seek. You won't find it anywhere else.

- The more at peace you are within, the better you'll pick up the pieces without.

- Walking the spiritual path on practical feet is a journey of spiritual orthopedics which fosters inner peace if we want to step confidently and lively toward Self-Realization. It doesn't matter if our steps are on bare feet or shoed feet, big feet or small feet, white feet or brown feet or red  feet, tired feet or energetic feet. Each step is a tithe toward our becoming one with our Divine Nature. The spiritual orthopedics of any truth walk requires steadfast faith, supported by love, wisdom, and zeal, multiplied by understanding and strength, and a penchant for divinely ordering every experience we have from the consciousness of our oneness with GOD, the Ground of All Beingness and Non-beingness.

- We believe, that in spite of your karmic baggage, you aren't here to learn specific lessons. However, while you're here you have an opportunity to lessen self-defeating learning.

- Religion has spiritual moments and spirituality has religious moments. That being said, we invite you to live each consecutive-moment-of-now in the light of spiritual awakening rather than in the darkness of religious dogma.

- You don't have to go to India, or Tibet, or recluse yourself on a mountaintop for a vision quest, or sit at the feet of a guru in an Ashram somewhere to find inner peace. All you need to do is go to the 'still point' (spiritual singularity) at the center of your being.

- There are no secret handshakes, passwords, or hoops to reach your Divine Nature – all you have to do is go into the Silence within.

- An 'I' for and 'i' will bring you the inner peace you seek. Why? Because the capital 'I' is your Y☯Universal Extraordinary Self and the small 'i' is your unenlightened egocentric nature.

- Inner peace is our clean and spacious 'Upper Room' – empty of unnecessary, antiquated, divinity-denying egocentric furnishings.

- Repeating the *'Oṃ maṇi padme hūṃ'* as a spiritual practice is a well-known six-syllabled Sanskrit mantra. *Om* is the sound of creation. *Mani* means 'jewel' or 'bead' and *Padma* means 'lotus flower, which is the Buddhist sacred flower. Our favorite translation is: *Om* purifies all of creation (all of the realms of the gods); *Ma* purifies jealousy and the need for self-aggrandizing entertainment (realm of the jealous gods); *Ni* purifies passion and desire (realm of human wants); *Pad* purifies ignorance and prejudice (realm of animal instincts); *Me* purifies selfishness and possessiveness (realm of the hungry ghosts); *Hum* purifies aggression and hatred (realm of a hellish state of consciousness). What's left without these realms of woe? Inner peace, of course!

> *Prosperous beliefs are like a mental shampoo. They'll wash the materialistic film off your thinking, being, and doing.*

- You'll enjoy the inner peace you seek when you Feng Shui your thoughts, choices and actions.
- Silent relaxation is a spiritual practice that helps you to, well, relax! It helps you attain a state of increased calmness, comfort, and composure. It calls for you to lie back on a couch or bed, close your eyes, and sleep or take a cat nap in a quiet room depending how much time you want to devote to the experience. It's sort of like a portable Sabbath (resting from worldly concerns and material wants).
- Always bring the poise of your Inner Light to the noise of outer circumstances.
- In a very real sense, a Gourmet Gospel is metaphysical, esoteric, theosophical, anthroposophical, allegorical, and metaphorical interpretations of the higher truths contained in the literal interpretations of the Gospels which can bring us the inner peace and clarity that lead to Self-Realization.
- MetaSpiritually, 'everlasting hell' means remaining in a hellish state of consciousness by refusing to acknowledge our innate divinity or choosing inner peace.

- Refrain from 'otherizing' yourself. Adopt a consciousness that isn't tied to the world of appearances. Realize that the only separation between you and your Y☯Universal Self is a consciousness of separation.

- In IT language, software that has been installed on a computer without the user's knowledge, consent, or control is called badware. Badware is a term used to describe error thoughts, choices and intentions that which are wearhoused in your subconscious and surface in your consciousness, catching you by surprise. To extend that analogy, badware is anything that compromises your inner peace. It includes the actions you take as a result of your thinking and the consequences you suffer as a result of your poor choices. It also takes into account a faulty world view, self-defeating beliefs and bad habits. It even includes interpersonal relationships that are detrimental to your well-being. Make a list of your most bothersome badware and prioritize the error thoughts, choices, habits and intentions you want to eliminate. Spend quality time on this practice.

- When you have inner peace you can avoid an view of the world.

- When you declare your independence from anything that limits or blocks your spiritual growth, unconditional love, compassion, and loving kindness for yourself and others, you'll achieve the inner peace you want.

- Delinquency, metaphorically speaking, is choosing gross materialism over our spiritual growth and/or settling for darkness over our enlightenment.

- Realize that peace of mind comes from listening to your heart!

- Recognize and honor the presence of the Sacred Divinity as the Ground of All Spiritual Beingness in everything your consciousness, emotions and body; other people; animals; fowl; plants; cells; molecules; subatomic particles; waterways; the air you breathe; mountains and valleys; etc.

- ☯ Whenever you say affirmations, visualize positive outcomes, and meditate, you're stepping out of powerlessness and vulnerability. You're becoming more "response-able."

- ☯ Know that when you truly have inner peace, the acne of outer appearances will have little power over you. The clearer your inner vision, the clearer will be the face you show the world.

- ☯ Grace is a term present in many traditional religions. It's defined as the result of a divine influence outside of you which bestows favor on you to sanctify you when you mess up, to inspire virtuous impulses within you, and to strengthen you in order to endure trials, tribulations, and temptations. MetaSpiritually, efficacious grace refers to your corrective next steps whether they're in the form of amended thoughts, edited choices, and/or ameliorated actions. It's efficacious because it re-causes your experience and saves you from the consequences of your errant thoughts, words and actions. The 'divine influence' is your Divine Nature within. It's your Higher Spiritual Self which gives you the wherewithal to give up the false for the truth. Efficacious grace helps to strengthen your alignment with your Divine Nature through conscious improvement and self-correction.

- ☯ Be affirmative prayer-conditioned. Being affirmative prayer-conditioned is habitually employing daily doses of prayer as a Y☯Universal Prosperity practice. It means being constantly and consistently prayed-up. It's a type of peaceful preventative maintenance: pre-praying every day; pre-praying events, tasks, and important decisions.

- Refrain from a religious exclusivity bias. A religious exclusivity bias is characterized by believing a particular faith tradition is the only way to salvation. Unfortunately, religion's exclusivity bias derails it from its more spiritual and mystical roots, and thus, its enlightenment value, if you really want to achieve inner peace at its deepest level. We invite you to be more inclusive in your thinking, being and doing when it comes to actualizing your Higher Spiritual Nature. Consider the best practices, rituals, teachings, ceremonies, and principles of other faith traditions that can enrich your own spiritual growth. This approach is an integrative path that enriches your current practice by expanding your enlightenment bandwidth. Besides the obvious best practices, many faith traditions have an esoteric side that will take you to higher realms of thought that not only deepen your faith, but show you that, at an esoteric level, all religions are more similar than different. Refraining from an exclusivity bias will accelerate your enlightenment and foster your inner peace potential, because you won't find yourself 'walled in' by the dogma of a particular faith tradition.

- Purposely spreading lies, falsehoods, dishonesty, disinformation, and fabrications is 'Pinocchio-ing around' and isn't going to lead to inner peace or anything else life-affirming.

- If you begin to find yourself desensitizing and becoming emotionally numbed by negative and upsetting news coverage, create the headspace you need by meditating your way into a state of inner peace.

- Inner peace is taking time to piece together your Y☯Universal higher consciousness qualities.

- If you're fanatically invested in complete safety, unadulterated security, and absolute certainty, you're a breadth of fresh air on a troubled planet.

- From a MetaSpiritual perspective, an Immaculate Conception (Immaculate Reception) is the divinely inspired result of our intuitive intelligence, love, and receptivity to our innate divinity being raised to their highest and purest spiritual essences so that we immaculately conceive a pure, inviolate thought that leads to inner peace.

Inner peace is tranquility, composure, and poise in the midst of chaos.

- You won't find inner peace in self-centeredness. The peace 'that passeth all misunderstanding' is only achieved through capital 'S' Self-centeredness (actualizing your Soul Signature qualities).

- When you truly have inner peace, the acne of outer appearances will have little power over you. The clearer your inner vision, the clearer will be the face you show the world.

- Y☯Universal Prosperity is going inside into the field of peace and tranquility within so you can become consciously one with your Divine Nature, the Extraordinary Y☯U. It's finding that inner peace in the midst of whatever is going on around you.

- Live on the cutting edge of higher consciousness thought, not on the dull edge of conformity.

- It's always best to move towards the light, even if you get a few bruises and scrapes along the way.

- You'll find that you won't allow the inertia of past skin school programming, accumulated subconscious patterns, and embedded theologies to dampen your inner peace when the current you has inner peace.

- Be *Theodidaktosic*! In Greek mystery schools, *theodidaktosis* means that every initiate was taught from within by his/her own inner God Essence in strict proportion to the degree with which the person has established Self Enlightenment. *Theodidaktosic* attentiveness, as a Y☯Universal Prosperity practice, means listening to the 'Still Small Voice' (the inner promptings of your Divine Nature). Therefore we invite you to honor the promptings of the 'Still Small Voice.' When the Spiritual You, the Universal You, decided to enter into another incarnational experience the 'Still Small Voice' capacity came with you. It's in your spiritual DNA. It's part of your divine connection and is manifested as intuitive intelligence.

- Another way of looking at an infant mortality rate is the number of newly formed spiritual ideas (infants) that 'die' in an egocentric consciousness every day and prevent you from experiencing inner peace.

- When you allow the age old patterns and tendencies of your negative karma to sabotage your inner peace, you're paying too high of a price to continue carrying them as baggage.

- Turn your negative karmic baggage into positive karmic luggage and you'll enjoy inner peace.

- When you're in the rarified air of Superconscious thought instead of the habitual negative subconscious patterns of your Human Nature, you'll enjoy being 'in joy.'

- Forgive yourself for carrying the negative karmic baggage you've accumulated throughout your past lifetimes – including this one; and forgive the negative karma for sticking around. You'll find the inner peace you seek has only been wedged between the karmic baggage you've just gotten rid of.

- Zen is a very Buddha-ful consciousness-raising spiritual practice. So, be very Zenful every chance you get. That means there are times when you must *go slow to go fast* – soooo, unhinge from adrenaline rushes that might cause you to plunge headlong into ruining relationships, making simple mistakes, cause accidents, etc. Remind yourself that infinite patience produces timely results in the long run!

- Each of our thoughts, words, and actions is a soul sequel. Unlike most movie sequels which are generally embarrassing attempts at movie-making, our soul sequels must continue to evolve and improve or remain re-makes of our error consciousness which is rooted in the depths of our subconsciousness during our reincarnational and incarnational experiences.

- Putting jigsaw puzzles together is a terrific mandala practice. Creating mandalas is a way of meditation that when used, with or without music or sound, is a means of centering your thoughts and emotions in a calming manner that fosters inner peace.

- Realize that you can move from worrier to warrior and victim to victor by right of consciousness.

- The job of your subconsciousness is to ensure that you respond exactly the way you've programmed yourself through many physical lifetimes. Your subconscious mind makes everything you think, say and do fit a pattern consistent with your accumulated self-concept. So, you have the power in this now moment to program the inner peace you want. How? Simply choose inner peace each-consecutive-moment-of-now.

- ☯ When there are no enemies within, the path toward Self-Realization and your Y☯Universal Prosperity is assured.

- ☯ We're doing time here (in skin school) because the *'Only Begotten'* has become the *'Only Forgotten!'* We've forgotten we're the biological addresses of the Life Force of GOD, the Omnipresent Universal Reality showing up through our Divine Nature in a human envelope *as* us.

- ☯ You're both ancestor and heir, host and guest, guru and student to your continued spiritual growth. You're not only a multi-storied spiritual being, you're a multi-dimensional quantum being. Knowing this is the peace 'that passeth all misunderstanding.'

- ☯ We're the Truth becoming *truthized* each-consecutive-moment-of-now.

- ☯ All of the world's great spiritual teachers have one thing in common. It doesn't matter who they are, where they're from, or in what era they lived. It includes the gurus and spiritual masters, both men and women, who preceded Yeshua (Jesus), the Buddha, Krishna, Lao Tzu, Black Elk, the 14th Dali Lama, Mother Teresa, Thich Nhat Hanh – and those who came before and will come after. In every case, the one distinct thing they have in common is - they spent their entire ministry in the same place. Sounds incredible doesn't it? But it's true. They have devoted all of their time and energy there. As do all great spiritual teachers. That place is a place we call the *'Subconscious Depot.'* It's our subconsciousness – the place where all of our human and interdimensional experiences, patterns of behavior, life scripts, faulty coping patterns, and egocentric defense mechanisms are wearhoused. And it's a place spiritual teachers have been trying to get humankind out of for centuries.

- Tame your amygdala (your fight, flight, freeze response to the world of outer appearances). Don't allow it to hijack your inner peace. Why? Because the amygdala's freight is fear, doubt, anger, anxiety, depression, hopelessness, psychosis, learned helplessness, insecurity, panic, and paranoia.

- Remind yourself that the proverbial Biblical Apocalypse is simply the unenlightened ego's derailment and not an end-of-the-world catastrophic event.

- See the Biblical 'burning bush' story as a metaphor for a Crown Chakra moment.

- Your subconscious mind is actively maneuvering behind the scenes to verify the thoughts, produce the emotions, and select the activities that'll move you closer to the reality that's most consistent with your evolutionary filter bubble. So, to enjoy the wealth, wellth, inner peace, security and happiness you want, you must Y☯Universalize your waking consciousness.

- Your personal ego (self-referent awareness) is an exquisite quantum instrument. You'll have an egocentric nature in each of your dimensions of being. Simply subordinate your sense consciousness to your Super-Consciousness in each dimension of being in which you find yourself.

- True inner peace is lasting peace, durable peace, resilient peace!

- Blend your superior intuition and intellect because the feminine potencies (negative energy) are centered in the Heart Chakra, which is the seat of your superior intuition. Your masculine potencies (positive energy) are centered in your Brow and Crown chakras, which are the seat of your intellect. Affirm the perfected body that will be the result of balancing both of these potent energies and nurture their alignment through higher conscious thoughts, feelings, exercise and diet.

- Enjoy 'me-time.' Planned and serendipitous timeouts are important. Selfcare sabbaticals are good for the soul.

> *Be aware that if you object to meditation and mindfulness, you're trivializing your enlightenment and minimizing your YOUniversal Prosperity.*

- Recognize that you'll receive apocalyptic insights (insights that forecast the end of the unenlightened ego's power to derail you from your spiritual growth) from time-to-time. These insights (Inner Guidance) lead to the extinguishment of your dependence on sense attachments. They project the attainment of your highly expansive spiritual consciousness and alchemicalized body which are the products of your YOUniversal inner peace.

- Connecting with your eternal Divine Nature by aligning your Human Nature with it is mojo rising (raising your spiritual octave).

- See mindfulness as a cognitive firewall that protects you from irrational thinking, ridiculous choices and preposterous actions.

- You'll go a long way toward establishing YOUniversal health, happiness, inner peace and financial freedom when you cut the following things out of your life: absurdity, aggrandizement, agitation, alcoholism, anger, bitterness, blind ambition, callousness, corruption, cruelty, demeaning comments, drug addiction, envy, excess, neglect, excuses, fear, filth, gluttony, greed, hatred, harshness, hostility, hypocrisy, idiocy, immorality, incompetence, indecency, insincerity, jealousy, laziness, litigation, littering, maliciousness, manipulation, materialism, narcissism, negativism, nit-picking, over-indulgence, paranoia, passivity, pessimism, prejudice, profanity, quarrelsomeness, resentment, redundancy, repugnancy, rhetoric, rudeness, scuzziness, self-centeredness, self-doubt, shortsightedness, snobbishness, substance abuse, thoughtlessness, tokenism, toxic behavior, underhandedness, unfounded suspicions, unsportsmanlike conduct, unnecessary pain, violence, wastefulness, wolfishness, egotistical workaholism, and spiteful yakkity-yak.

- ☯ Each spiritual thought, every Y☯Universally-centered intention, each step into your Superconscious awareness moves your entire beingness into peaceful at-one-ment with your Divine Nature.

- ☯ Eve symbolizes superior intuition and your potential to feeeeel and expressss your feelings about sensory experience in skin school. For example, the 'conversation' between 'Eve and the serpent' is the dialogue going on in your head as you try to summon the courage to awaken the kundalini energies within on your quest for enlightenment. That kind of 'internal conversation' (Idaic Life Force) will increase the bandwidth of your intuitive perspective and bring you inner peace.

- ☯ Adam symbolizes the archetypical movement in mind that epitomizes the reasoning, reductionist, objective, logical, deductive, methodical and judgmental nature of our make-up. Adamic energies (manifesting as the pingalic Life Force channel or *nadi*) underwrite our left brain-ness and are very much tied to our thoughts. It's this pingalic Life Force that can bring us to the doorway of superior reasoning.

- Know that when you live, move and have your being from a state of Y☯Universal Prosperity, you're in the *flow* of life because you're 'practicing the Presence' of the Extraordinary Y☯U.

Meditate daily so you can specialize in heart-to-head resuscitation.

- Affirm: "Because I live at the speed of my Y☯Universal Consciousness, I enjoy incredible health, happiness, inner peace, and financial freedom in all areas of my life."

- Tactfully, and to your own satisfaction, take care of unresolved issues that sap your energy and compromise your inner peace. You'll feel a ton of emotional weight lifted off your shoulders.

- Collect positive, inspiring, motivational, and riveting quotes that deepen your spirituality, broaden your peacemaking and humanitarian perspectives, advocate health and wellness, enhance your connection with the Authentic You, and help you become a better person. Collect your sound bites from A to Z in a file. Refer to them often. Keep especially meaningful and inspiring bytes on your iphone and iPad, in your purse or wallet. Post them in your home and office. Refer to them when you've had a rough day or just want to be motivated. Come up with powerful sound bites of your own.

- Honor your BS. Before your lower jaw drops too far – the 'BS' we're talking about stands for your '**B**elief **S**ystem.' After all, it's all BS, right! It's the story we tell ourselves to define our personal sense of 'reality.' Every human being has a belief system that he/she lives by, and it's through this world view that we try to make sense of the world around us. We can even call our 'BS' the Theory of Everything (a quantum physics term that attempts to describe the nature of the universe). Regardless of what you individually believe, honor your belief system if you're convinced that your particular beliefs are the correct ones. At the same time it asks you to remain open to credible 'evidence' that surfaces which prompts you to change, modify, refine or enhance your current belief system.'

- We believe there'll be peace on earth when people the world over have the courage and inner peacefulness to face the most inconvenient spiritual truth of all time. It's amazing at the lengths traditional Christian teachings have gone to down play the following universal truth of all time: The 'Only Begotten' born in a manger to Joseph and Mary is the same 'Only Begotten' born as each of us. The 'Only Begotten' is the Cosmic Logos (Primordial Vibration, Eternal Universal Pulse) actualizing Itself through our Divine Nature *as* us in human form.

- People who have a high degree of inner peace know that the proverbial expression that asks whether the glass is half empty or half full are missing the point: the glass is refillable!

- No crucifixion (crossing out error), no Self-Realization.

- When you're aligned with your Soul Signature Essence, you can "order up" the divine ideas, intuitive guidance, and resources you need for your spiritual highest and best, to move through life with grace, inner peace, and joy.

- In the wisdom traditions, the Third Eye is the gateway to higher consciousness, and thus enlightenment. The Third Eye is often associated with clairvoyance, precognition, astral visions, out-of-body experiences, and astral travel (astral aeronautics). These inner 'knowings' are not clouded by egotistical thoughts, intentions or assumptions. They're instinctual messages that arise in you, seemingly from nowhere and often run in opposition to your rational thoughts. Soooo, follow your intuitive compass. Trust it. Its guidance is pure and its timing is exquisite.

A prosperity consciousness, like a field ready for an abundant crop, needs cultivation.

- Divinely ordering your good is a conscious process of allowing your prosperity to flow through you. It's affirming your good. It's recognizing that Divine Substance is available to you each-consecutive-moment-of-now from the Field of Infinite Potential!
- Recognize that *lackology* and *limitology* are merely human inventions.
- Have absolutely zero doubt that we're pre-wired for abundance. Abundance is part of our spiritual 'up-bringing.'
- Be aware that you attract or repel what you want or need by the quality of your thinking, being and doing.
- Remind yourself that you can manifest anything you want when you raise your thought vibrations to the bandwidth needed to collapse the unlimited waves of potentiality into their respective ideational counterparts and follow that up with

spirited choices and actions. That means 'upping your consciousness' into the rarified air of Y☯Universal Thought which defines your Transcendent Spiritual Nature. That means completely trust in and identify with your Homo Deus Nature.

- ☯ Recognize that there's no lid on what you can create. The secret is to know what you want. As you move forward on your own journey, and as you create your next chapter, take time to go into the Silence. Be still, and then determine what you want the future to look like for you! When you've done all of that, INVENT your future!

- ☯ Many prosperity teachers shout, "Just hold the right thought and you can get (attract, magnetize) anything you want." Their theme is *get, get, get*. True 'prosperity shaping' is holding the right thought so you can GIVE, GIVE, GIVE anything you want! And you do that by creating the inner peace that comes from Y☯Universal Prosperity.

- ☯ Pay attention to your intuitive thoughts which remind you that what you think often enough, what you say often enough, and what you do often enough determine the degree of inner peace you'll enjoy.

- ☯ Don't concern yourself about unmanifested good. Right thoughts and actions help move possibilities into probabilities and hidden potentials into physical realities.

- ☯ YouTube a 3-minute clip called the *Samurai and the Fly*. It's a fantastic piece about staying centered in the midst of chaos.

- ☯ Here's the truth about lack and limitation: they exist because we believe there're going to exist. Consequently, we don't do what we can do to manifest what we want. Lack and limitation's existence is merely up to us.

- It's a myth that you must magnetize your good to yourself. The truth is your good is already available to you in the Field of Infinite Potential. Therefore, you don't magnetize your good *to* you! Realize that your good doesn't come *to* you, it comes *through* you. That's the true directionality.

Remember six little words that'll help you stay sane and centered in a topsy turvy world:
Do one thing at a time.

- You can affirm all you want, storyboard all you want, visualize all you want, pray and meditate 24-7, and act as if the objects of your desires are already there, BUT, if you put whims of your unenlightened egocentric nature ahead of superior discernment of your Divine Nature, you'll dam up the flow and contaminate your inner peace.

- Minimize being preoccupied with things that don't matter, circumstances that cause you to confuse activity with accomplishment, routines that cause you to major in minor things.

- Focus your attention on the things you can control. And the number one thing you can control is your life. Few things are more disconcerting than living out of alignment with your true spiritual nature.

- Inner peace is like a clean and spacious house - empty of unnecessary, worthless, cumbersome, superfluous, surplus and broken emotional stuff. MetaSpiritually speaking, a house stands for our consciousness. So, it makes sense to have a consciousness that's not filled with debilitating thoughts and emotions.

- Procrastination creates cumulative emotional baggage that can drag you down. So, hesitate to hesitate when you know you need to get something done. Be unflappable in your responses to things you know you can take care of. That's being response-able.

- Recognize that no one can push your buttons without your consent. Actually, if the truth be told, and we believe we're telling you the truth - you have no buttons to push. None of us have 'buttons' like that unless we manufacture them. The closer you get to making inner peace one of your core attributes, the more you'll realize that what we're saying is true.

- Everyone has faults and little things they don't like about themselves. So, embracing the good, the bad, the beautiful and the ugly about yourself can be both enlightening and sobering. Eliminate the you's about you that you've outgrown and nurture the you's you want to keep. That self-development process itself will bring you inner peace.

- Experiencing inner peace is piecing together the important parts of the Inner You and the outer you, the Extraordinary You and the ordinary you, the Wise You and the *'Whys you'* that seeks answers.

- Someone once told us that the way to achieve enduring inner peace is to finish what we start. So, after hearing that advice, Cher finished her second cup of pumpkin spice coffee, and Bil finished his candy bar of dark chocolate. We both felt contented and peaceful immediately.

- Declutter your thought universe. Do not indulge in any thought that attacks your self-worth or denies your innate divinity.

- Inner peace is extraordinarily medicinal. It lowers blood pressure, reduces anxiety by lowering the levels of blood lactate, helps in post-operative healing, enhances the immune system, drops cholesterol levels, cures headaches, increases serotonin levels, and increases vitality, to name a few of its highly therapeutic effects. It's literally a pharmacy of rejuvenation.

- Look in the mirror and ask the person you see: "Have you crossed over yet?" It's a question that defines where you are on your spiritual journey. The 'crossing over' we're referring to isn't in the context of near death experiences, out-of-the-body experiences, or psychic readings and séances. Although that's generally what the question above refers to when it comes to paranormal human experiences. The 'crossing over' we're referring to is this – "Have you crossed over yet … from a dogmatic religious mindset into a more open-minded spiritual mindset? Have you moved from a religious perspective that's based on fear, guilt and shame, or have you adopted a spiritual perspective that celebrates your innate goodness and worthship as a spiritual being in human form?" One perspective leads to inner strife. The other leads to inner peace.

- Possessing phenomenal material wealth and more money than you can spend, without inner peace, is like dying of thirst while you're standing in a mountain lake.

- By practicing kind acts toward others, you're creating a kindness-aware inner climate that fosters your own inner peace and soul contentment. Being kind to others is being kind to yourself!

- Affirm the Third Coming. The Third Coming occurs when you become fully Self-Realized. When that happens your inner peace will create peace in your world.

- Stop shoulding on yourself – and on others. And by all means, stop wasting excessive psychological energy on anger, resentment, insecurity, unforgiveness, and the other heavy baggage that an unhealthy ego retails. When you eliminate those toxic patterns, you'll find that you have more time and energy available for love, inner peace, happiness, bliss, and calmness.

- Be kind to animals. By the way, MetaSpiritually speaking, animals represent our basic human instincts. So, spiritualize your basic instincts through your husbandry with animals. All animals deserve to be treated humanely - family pets and wildlife. Create an inviting space in your yard and garden for butterflies, squirrels, hummingbirds and other creatures. While animals like deer, bats, skunks, squirrels and raccoons can be a nuisance, look for ways to coexist with animals as well as protect your property humanely.

- Choose your digital entertainment carefully. Watch TV, movies, and YouTubes that are wholesome and have a positive, uplifting message. Read books and other printed material that are wholesome as well.

- Inner peace is built on positive affirmations. Every time you say a positive affirmation, each time you engage in positive self-talk, every time you insert positive feelings and perspectives into painful, limiting states of mind – you build new neural pathways. Over time, the accumulating impact of this positive material will, synapse by synapse, neuroplastize your brain in positive, life-affirming ways, helping you achieve the inner peace you seek.

- Explore the world of dreams as a highly credible divine connection and inner peace mechanism. Dreams are nocturnal messages from ourselves to ourselves. Some are prophetic, others call for emotional and physical growth and transformation. Still others are warnings to clean up our human acts. Many are re-enactments from the day's activities. Dreams are truly one of our magic mirrors toward self-recovery and actualization. The power of dreams to support your quest for inner peace are legendary.

- Grace is a term present in many religions. It's defined as the divine influence which operates in you to regenerate and sanctify you when you mess up, to inspire virtuous impulses within you, and to strengthen you in order to endure trials, tribulations, and temptations. MetaSpiritually, grace refers to your own corrective next steps whether they're in the form of amended thoughts, edited choices, and/or ameliorated actions. And it's efficacious grace that re-causes your experience and saves you from the consequences of your errant thoughts, words and actions.

- Don't hesitate to employ *tyagaian* releases. *Tyagaian* release is a term from the Bhagavad Gita that literally means 'to abandon anything that hinders your enlightenment.'

☯ Inner peace leads to demonstrable acts of kindness – and demonstrable acts of kindness lead to inner peace. There are many ways of coming full circle. For example:

Cook a healthy meal for someone, clean a friend's house, give some change to another customer to help pay for his/her purchase, thank your bus or taxi driver, deliver a dessert to firefighters and/or school teachers, help a child start a piggy bank, help someone find a job, mow a senior citizen's lawn, pay someone's parking meter before it expires, leave Post-it Notes with inspirational messages on them for colleagues to see, send someone an eCard, spend time with someone who needs someone who'll listen, buy someone a book, write a positive blog post, praise someone, give a homeless person something to wear, show compassion to someone you may dislike, send notes of appreciation, give money to down-and-out people on the side of the road, be generous with compliments, say 'Bless you' when someone sneezes, post inspirational quotes on your Facebook page, help someone financially, pet-sit for someone, email a quick note to a friend who needs to 'hear' a kind word, let someone go in line in front of you, take a photo of people who want to capture a vacation moment together, wash someone's car, give theatre tickets away for free, shovel snow for a neighbor, tip big for extraordinary customer service, treat a friend to some fresh fruit, politely let another driver merge in front of you, call a friend who's sick, give a napkin folded into a rose to a waitress for her excellent service.

- Add *zamzummim* actions to your Y☯Universal Prosperity happiness resume. In Hebrew terms, *zamzummims* were a race of giants in Canaan. *Zamzummim* actions involved the act of pondering and/or reflecting on something spiritually expansive, far-reaching and huge. For example, affirming world peace, seeing an end to hunger, working toward an end to violence and war, maintaining a vigil for the humane treatment of animals, soldiering to help humankind become more spiritual than religious, and joining others to support an end to global warming – are all *zamzummim* actions.

- Realize that there's no shortcut to enlightenment no matter how fast you want to get there. Your position (your current skin school experience) only has a certain amount of velocity (spiritual awareness). Honor your present moment existence and strive to be the best Y☯Universal Y☯U you can be. You're already immortal – and your current immortal position is where the cumulative you has gotten you so far. So, relax and enjoy the trip!

- We invite you to master both the inner and the outer game of *well*th management.

- March 21st is the World Day for Inner Peace. Yes, there's actually a global day to awaken the world to celebrate a world without conflict or chaos. We invite you to celebrate that day – actually everyday – as a day of inner peace.

- Don't hang around with people who inflate disturbing news into hysteria-laden Armageddons. Express your concerns and fears to trusted friends who are just as concerned as you are, but who see more optimistic and positive outcomes. These are friends who anesthetize negativity, kick fear-mongering to the curb, and have a more positive outlook on life.

- ☯ Be willing to purge purgatory. MetaSpiritually speaking, what's known as the traditional ecclesiastical purgatory is the stagnant pool of worldly thoughts, toxic thinking patterns, and ingrained beliefs about ourselves that are stuck in the negative regions of our subconsciousness (purgatory) which aren't quite ready to be morphed (percolate up into our waking consciousness) into their higher spiritual, more life-affirming essences.

Calm the unquiet city. The unquiet city is the unenlightened egocentric human consciousness.

- ☯ Enjoy spiritual tourism. The spiritual tourism we're referring to encourages you to sample many, if not all, of the hundredths of spiritual practices our Global Center For Spiritual Practices has to offer and return to your main spiritual practice with 'souvenirs' (our spiritual practices) that you want to add to your own soul development resume. We believe many of these practices will be included in your list of favorite 'places to go (adopt)' – every day, every week, every month. Some will be regular 'stops' on your spiritual path. Others will be considered as once in a lifetime journeys. Whatever your experience, you'll see that these practices are for people who consider themselves to be more spiritual than religious.

- ☯ Be thought-conscious on your way to achieving the uninterrupted prosperity you want. Rule out failure thoughts, thoughts that shrink your inner peace, and thoughts that doubt your being able to thoroughly enjoy the ease and comfort of a peaceful thought Y☯Universe.

- Universal Supply is constantly available in the Field of Infinite Potential, and it is within your thinking, knowledge, use of technology, willpower, and reach to achieve the Y☯Universal prosperity you visualize. Until you believe that, you won't experience the inner peace you need for achieving the uninterrupted prosperity and abundance you seek.

- Inner peace debugs resentment, anger, unforgiveness, bitterness, grudges, huffiness, irritation, animosity, etc.

- Inner peace is an hourly, daily, weekly, monthly, and yearly mindfulness process. It's a piecing together of peaceful moments each-consecutive-moment-of-now.

- Inner peace is cultivating inner tranquility in spite of the restlessness and chaos that characterize the world of outer appearances.

- Peace *of* mind is generally precipitated by months, and years, and lifetimes of peace *in* mind.

- Inner peace helps us enter every 'now moment' peacefully, tranquilly and serenely.

- Inner peace occurs when you do the right thing based on what's moral, ethical, decent and virtuous when it comes to the common good of all concerned. It means never compromising foundational humanitarian and spiritual principles for the presumed expediency of the moment.

- When you confidently handle anything - anything - in life that comes your way, you'll experience the inner peace that soothes any suffering, hardship, anguish and adversity.

- Peace on earth from a MetaSpiritual perspective, means having enduring tranquility (inner peace) as the foundation that defines our waking consciousness (earth).

- Inner peace leads to calmness ... Calmness results in inner peace ... Inner peace leads to calmness ... *(repeat)*
- Whether you seek national peace or global peace or inner peace or a combination of all three, the way to experience its therapeutic effects is to strengthen the conscious alignment between your Human Nature and your Divine Nature.

Inner peace is forgiving people even when they're not sorry.

- Liberation from all types of confinement, confusion, coercion, constraint, and captivity is the essence of the handcuff-busting power of inner peace.
- When you think about it, inner peace is an inside job!
- I have the serenity to accept whatever I'm unable to change, the courage and stick-to-it-tiveness to change the things I can, and the intuitive wisdom to know the difference.
- Adamant *thingumajigging* is a great inner peace spiritual practice. And here's why. It means casting off a part of us that doesn't contribute to our Greater Good - things like lack of confidence, bad habits, debilitating addictions, recurring doubts, chronic fears, and negative attitudes – you know, things that minus us.
- A collection of dogmatic religious beliefs, unruly faith-based inclinations, unscrupulous theological thoughts, or unsettling pontifical intentions in your thought universe won't bring you the inner peace you seek. We call those things a cranky thought congregation.

- Inner peace comes the moment you choose to become one with your Divine Nature.
- We're password protected because we have immediate access to the greatest security system in the world: the Still Small Voice which is the Soundless Voice of our Soul Signature. And the password is: *Peace be still.*

Spiritual Practice:
4-7-8 Breathing

Use the incredible 4-7-8 breathing technique. It's a perfect prep for becoming peaceful.

Here's How This Practice Works:

Focus on the following breathing pattern:

- Inhale quietly through your nose for 4 seconds.
- Hold your breath for a count of 7 seconds.
- Exhale forcefully through pursed lips by making a 'whoosh' sound, to a count of 8 seconds.
- Repeat that inhalation/exhalation pattern 3 times in succession. It's an excellent technique for entering a peaceful state of being.

– Financial Freedom Matters –

The Financial Freedom Matters teachings we share are based on how well we manage our relationship with material wealth, status, money, and power so we can achieve the lifelong financial independence and security we seek through healthy earnings, savings, investments, and philanthropic pursuits.

Are you ready for some Money-related Y☯Universal Prosperity Hors d'oeuvres? Let's dig in!

- Many people ask: "If money were no object, what would I do?" The thing is – money IS an object! It's one of the chief currencies in skin school. There's a need to make money – a certain amount of money to live comfortably and prosperously! So, a better question to ask yourself might be: "Knowing I need to attract a certain amount of income to maintain the lifestyle I want, what can I do to accomplish that?"
- MONEY is an acronym! It stands for: **M**y **O**wn **N**irvanic **E**nergy **Y**ield.
- Remember the Y☯Universal Prosperity Principle of Mind Action: Thoughts and feelings held in mind produce similar thoughts and feelings in your thought universe. So, put positive and practical thoughts in your mental bank.

Realize that you are rich in direct proportion to that which you can do without.

- Opt for unlimited Y☯Universal Prosperity, and limit or eliminate as much credit card debt as possible.
- Remind yourself that wealth isn't the same thing as income.
- Here's the thing: if you make a good income and spend it all, you aren't getting wealthier! Monetary wealth is what you accumulate, not what you spend.
- The economics of prosperity means you have ready access to the omnipresent supply of Universal Substance. You have access to unlimited prosperity through Y☯Universal Harmony. The only deposits you have to make are faith, positive affirmations, and belief in your ability to manifest.

- Get the concept of 'seeing is believing' out of your thought universe. *'Believing financial security is seeing financial security'* is a better perspective.

- Spend no more than a third of your take-home pay on housing to leave room for other financial goals, such as paying down debt, saving and investing, and fun.

- The whole concept behind abundance and prosperity is that our universal spiritual substance never runs dry. It's always funded. We're constantly capitalized. There's no limitation – only a *consciousness* of limitation.

- Hyper-focusing on making money, getting money, keeping money, spending money, investing money, and hoarding money may make you feel financially wealthy, but could very well contribute to your mental, emotional, physical and spiritual bankruptcy.

- People's issues with money is really a consciousness of scarcity, the belief in lack, that everything is in limited supply. And it isn't just about money and material things; it also relates to beliefs about fulfilling work, the perfect relationship, friends you can trust, etc. This faulty mindset affects both rich and poor, and leads to mistrust, exploitation, manipulation, envy, stinginess, and a host of other negative reactions, including the perspective that ceaseless acquisition is the best way to live.

- Prosperity follows the lines of least resistance. So, stop resisting financial leverage by doubting your innate ability to manifest your financial security by right of consciousness.

- Avoid taking cash advances on one credit card to pay off another one.

- You're pre-wired for abundance. Abundance is very definitely part of your spiritual DNA. Have faith in your innate Divine connection. Have faith that your financial liquidity is only one thought, one affirmation, one Divinely-inspired action away.

- Never make an assertion, no matter how true it may look on the surface, that you don't want to see manifest in your life. Re-read that sentence! It forces you to be really aware of what you're thinking, saying, and doing. Even something as simple as "I'm not good with money." Or "I'm broke." You don't want to see those financial pitfalls manifest, so don't say them! Become aware of what you're thinking and saying to yourself.

- When discouragement besets you, and your deepest longing about prosperity feels in vain, affirm: Every day in every way, I'm growing more prosperous in health matters, happiness matters, inner peace matters, and money matters.

- Dare to be serious about money matters, if you want prosperous monetary dividends to seriously manifest for you. Money is the means of exchange in this skin school – so learn and understand the principles related to it.

- The best way to make money is to let your money make money for you. That means being able to live off the money your money makes, rather than off the sweat of your brow.

- Enduring financial fitness means saving at least 10% of your annual income every year. This is investing in yourself!

- Don't make extra payments on your home mortgage. Put that extra money in a savings account, invest it, and/or put it in a self-funded retirement fund.

- There is a hydraulic relationship between lack consciousness and lack of opportunities. The greater our lack consciousness, the fewer opportunities we'll have to create the prosperity we seek. You'll 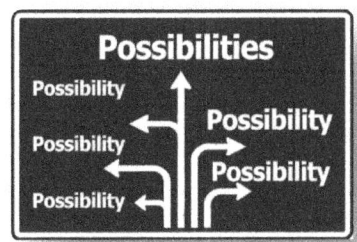 be surprised how people never miss an opportunity to miss an opportunity. The truth is, opportunities don't come *to* us – they come *through* us! And they are abundant!

- We're going to toss two questions at you as attention getters in terms of money matters: Is your consciousness filled with pockets of resistance or pockets of plenty when it comes to money? Is it lined with *self-interest* or *interest* in philanthropy?

- Grow your disposable income by pulling the weeds of over-consumptive spending, and then pruning unhealthy lifestyle spending habits.

- Steer clear of the so called 'hottest stocks' everyone is touting mindlessly, the ones whose companies are diversifying into areas that aren't connected to their core business strengths, and those who supply most of their products and services to one or a very limited customer base.

- In the midst of experiencing an "ebb" rather than a "flow," continue to believe in your future prosperity. Focus on abundance rather than lack. Pay gladly to reduce your credit card  debt. Forgive yourself if you feel badly about the debt you've incurred. Give thanks for your worthiness to manifest your Greater Good. We actually write the word "Gladly" above the "Pay to the order of.." line on our checks! People notice!

- When you're choosing a financial planner, look for one who is a certified fee-only professional affiliated with one or more of these financial organizations: The National Association of Personal Financial Advisors, Garrett Financial Network, and The Alliance of Cambridge Advisors. They are all credible alliances of fee-only financial advisors.

- We believe possessing material possessions is okay as long as they don't possess us. Money and possessions are fine. We have a nice house and a nice car. Bil is attached to Cher, golf, jigsaw puzzles, Y☯Universal Harmony, and writing. Cher is attached to Bil, coffee, ballroom dancing, Candy Crush, Paris, her Apple computers, and Y☯Universal Harmony as well. The important thing is not to allow material *things* to hold you hostage. They're fine as long as they don't hold your Y☯Universal Prosperity as collateral.

- Economize your thoughts. Fill your mental bank with positive, prosperity-oriented thoughts and affirmations. Delete negative, error-prone thinking from your thought ledger. As you elevate your financial abundance  consciousness, there are things you need to let go of, attitudes you need to grow out of, beliefs about money you need to compost, assumptions you need to re-cycle.

- Declare as often as necessary: "I purge all thoughts of lack and insufficiency from my consciousness, and veto any and all notions of my unworthiness and inability to manifest my financial security.

- Budgeting your monetary and material abundance is a prosperity plan for living beneath your yearnings.

- Recognize that abundance is the energy of permission. The more you permit yourself to honestly desire what you want and express gratitude for what you have, the more you'll find joy in manifesting whatever you want.

- Build a basic emergency fund. Having a small savings buffer in place is crucial for protecting yourself against emergency setbacks, such as unexpected car repairs or medical expenses. An emergency fund of 3-6 months will keep you prosperous.

- Know that filling your consciousness with more affirmative prayer, meditation, mindfulness, positive affirmations, and thoughts about financial security is prosperity shaping. It'll get you past the 'LULL' of attraction. It'll take you past the 'LULL' between manifesting something and waiting for what you want to manifest.

- The lack of money is the root of all upheaval.

- Constantly affirm: "I'm one with my Divine Nature, and I live joyfully, faithfully, philanthropically, and lovingly at the speed of my Y☯Universal Consciousness.

- Spiritual ECHO-nomics is a phrase we use to describe that what we send out comes back to us, multiplied! So, we invite you to create echoes in your financial management plan that are positive, prosperous, and congruent with both the spiritual principles and sound money management principles you know.

- Understand that you'll attract awesome financial prosperity when you confidently and consistently "practice the Presence" of funding your Divine Nature with thoughts of generosity and altruism.

- Banish toxic money thoughts. This is important because it's based on a self-fulfilling prophecy! If you psych yourself out by affirming such things as "I'll never pay off debt" or "I'm not very good at managing money" – you're setting yourself up to fail. So don't be a fiduciary fatalist.

Never, ever confuse your net worth with your self-worth!

- Don't be vague, apologetic, or hesitant about money unless you want money to be vague, apologetic, and hesitant about coming to you. Money is only one of the channels in which abundance flows through you. Once you align yourself with your Y☯Universal Nature, all financial channels will be open to you and money will flow to you freely, so that you'll have plenty to share and plenty to spare.

- Most people become millionaires not by inheriting money or winning millions in the lottery, but by earning a decent income from work they enjoy, living and spending below their means, and investing their savings wisely.

- Release and emphatically erase any and all negative thoughts, attitudes, and habits about money which you have allowed to limit or block your Greater Good.

- Neglecting your Y☯Universal Prosperity by favoring your unenlightened egocentric nature will block your prosperity dividends.

- Failing to use the abundance-accelerating power of *feeeeeling* the essence of unmanifested financial security will delay its manifestation.

- Retirement's an expensive prospect, so much so that most seniors need about 70% to 80% of their former income to maintain a decent lifestyle. Social Security generally provides about half that amount for anyone who's an average wage-earner. However, the rest of that retirement income needs to be generated elsewhere, and for those who don't have pensions, personal savings can fill that void. As of this writing, we recommend saving at least 15-20% of your income.

- Institute a 'no-buy' week each month. Other than necessities, intentionally spend zero money for a whole week. No eating out, no take-out coffee, no cinema outings, no new clothes, no spontaneous purchases, etc. The amount of money you'll save over a year will surprise you. Make this simple practice part of your financial literacy. (Note: The money we saved using this strategy generated the required down-payment for our first single-family home!)

- Make sure your certified financial advisors have kept up with the latest tax reform legislation. If they haven't, no matter what the excuse, it's time to get someone new!

- Believe it or not, one of the greatest money-making opportunities of tomorrow is in areas of the marketplace that don't even exist today! New technologies and services based on new ideas, that reduce the costs of what it takes to produce a new innovation – in any field – create demand that wasn't there before.

- When you think about it, most income isn't distributed – it's hard earned money.

- Add occasional spending fasts to your money management diet. Frivolous spending is a bad financial habit.

- Spending less than your take-home pay is a key Y☯Universal Prosperity practice.

- Humankind's unhealthy attachment to material wealth, status, money, power, and prestige has enslaved millions of people to the lure of outer appearances. Don't allow your tendency toward gold fever to leave you with lead feet when it comes to choosing spirituality over materiality.

- Lack consciousness comes from an anesthetized awareness of the omnipresence of a healthy portfolio of financial ideas housed in the Field of Infinite Potential (Garden of Eden). It's time to wake up!

- MetaSpiritually speaking, the Judeo-Christian concept of the Lord's Supper symbolizes the conscious union between our Human Nature and our Divine Nature. A sort of spiritual alchemy takes place as symbolized by the bread and wine. And it takes place in the Upper Room, which signifies a high state of spiritual consciousness. When we're in an 'Upper Room' state of consciousness, we have the wisdom to know the difference between sacred truths and falsehoods. We know the difference between the centrifugal force of materiality and the pull of Spirit.

- Neuro-science has given us neuro-theology. We believe the two will marry, and along with quantum physics, will give us a trinity of higher thought that will shake the foundations of pediatric religions which base their concept of prosperity on the whims of a vengeance-oriented, anger-prone, manipulative, anthropomorphic god meme who demands your tithes to his churches.

- Recognize that attachments are ornamental reactions to something we feel we need to complete us. Felt abundance is the recognition that we're already whole at the level of Spirit. We need *no thing* to complete us. It's the attachment to things which depletes us. So, celebrate your innate prosperous nature.

- You can improve your credit score faster and pay down your debt at the same time by asking your credit card company for a higher limit. Some companies will do this with a 'soft pull' on your credit, meaning you won't get dinged for it. Say you have a $5,000 limit across all your cards and you currently have a balance of $4,500. That means your current credit usage is 90%. If you can get your credit card(s) to raise your limit so you have a total of, say, $7,000, then your credit usage will drop to 64% before you've even made a dent with your payments. However, you'll want to keep your usage below 30% and ideally below 10%. So, if you can increase your limit **and** lower your usage, it will increase your credit score.

- Your composite material and monetary wealth is directly proportional to your Y☯Universal *well*th.

- Establish a credit mix. Your mix of credit sources should happen organically. Credit bureaus want to see that you can handle different types of debt. There are two basic types of credit that can affect your mix, revolving credit and installment credit. Revolving credit includes your credit cards and store cards. Installment credit includes any student loans, car loans, and mortgages.

- Everyone has a head, but not everyone uses their head or gets ahead when it comes to financially prosperous living.

- Prosperity is a way of thinking, feeling, and living, and not just having money and things. Poverty is a way of thinking, feeling, and living, and not just having money and things. So, be mindful of which of these polarities you're buying into, so you're on the life-affirming side of life.

- When it comes to material things, live below your over-consumptive yearnings.

- Keep credit inquiries low. Each time a creditor pulls your report, it'll get listed on your credit report. If you have more than two in a year, this can have a detrimental effect on your score. Trying to make too much credit available to yourself in a short amount of time makes credit bureaus antsy. If you're shopping around for a loan for a major purchase, apply to lenders within a short period of time (no more than a week or two). This tells credit bureaus that you're looking for a specific type of loan.

- When we served in our pulpit ministry we invited our congregation to tip rather than tithe. And here's why! Most people tithe 5-10%. However, tippers generally tip 18-20%. Do the math.

- Virtually all the blocks to your financial wealth are rooted in subconscious issues. By definition, you're unaware of things in your subconscious. The only way you become aware of them is when they manifest through your conscious thoughts, words, and actions. So it makes sense to begin to pay serious attention to your financial thoughts, words, and actions, so you can identify the useless monetary baggage you're carrying around in your subconscious, and defund it!

- You are pedigreed Infinite Isness, Transcendental Allness, Eternalness, and Cosmic Consciousness in human form. So, it's okay to build your financial portfolio unabashedly and without regret, just as much as you improve your health, happiness, and inner peace.

- One of the quickest ways to gain the wisdom of financial abundance and an abundance of financial wisdom is to walk the spiritual path with financial wherewithal and a well-funded financial portfolio.

☯ As a matter of spiritual financial fact, your wealth is never more than a thought away! It's closer than objects that appear in your rearview mirror. It's as close as your next breath. It's as close as your next thought, intention, word, choice, or action. It's as close as the book (or eBook) you're holding. It depends on how Y☯Universally Prosperous you think!

☯ If you're having less than perfect experiences in your finances, your relationships, your work, your health, your attitude, your life ~ recognize it's simply an outer manifestation of what's going on in your subconscious. You have the power to turn negative subconscious material into positive, life-affirming conscious thoughts, choices, and actions concerning your finances.

Let your money make more money! Invest as much money as you can in things that consistently earn you money.

☯ An orphaned tiger cub is raised by a benign herd of mild-mannered goats in their vegetarian ways. There are two questions which beg to be asked: Does the tiger remain naively satisfied with salads, bleating gratefulness for his daily fare? Or, one day, will he realize that just because he lives among mellowed-out, docile goats, he's not a goat? You may live and work around people who don't know how to manage money. That doesn't mean you don't have the Midas touch when it comes to a stronger financial portfolio.

☯ Affirm regularly: "I'm one with my Divine Nature and have such *heir* power that I attract and enjoy unlimited abundance."

- The real 'prosperity gospel' isn't underwritten by an anthropomorphic god in the sky who has human qualities. It's underwritten by the Omnipresent Universal Reality which is the Ground of All Beingness and Non-Beingness.

- We all receive *in*formation at the rate of 500 billion bits per second. What really matters is the *out*formation – what you *do* with the *in*formation which is ground zero for your Y☯Universal Prosperity? Conduct a personal audit on your *in*formation (what you're allowing to enter) and your *out*formation (how you are using it)! Make any necessary changes!

- Every time you experience the acoustics of financial abundance, it's because you've experienced the acoustics of sound money management.

- If you're considering closing some of your credit cards after they're paid off, close the newer cards. Keep your oldest card(s) open. Credit bureaus like to see an average credit length of at least 5-7 years, so if you close your older credit cards, this could adversely affect your score.

- Your alignment with your Divine Nature is the Source of your good – not governments, or banks, or Wall Street, or the economy, or employers, or economic indicators.

The economics of spirituality means you have ready access to unlimited prosperity through the Field of Infinite Potential. The only deposits you have to make are faith, patience, and trust in your innate ability to manifest what you want by right of consciousness.

- Spiritual economics is prosperity shaping.

- Move beyond the centrifugal force of outer appearances, which decry lack and limitation, by aligning your Human Nature with your Y☯Universal Self, the Extraordinary Y☯U.

- The whole concept behind spiritual economics is that your spiritual bank account never runs dry. It's always funded. You're constantly capitalized. There's no limitation – only a consciousness of limitation.

- Become wealthier every day in money matters. You'll be able to live prosperously each-consecutive-moment-of-now from your Y☯Universal Consciousness.

- Economize your thoughts. Fill your mental bank with positive, spiritually-oriented thoughts and affirmations. Delete negative, error-prone thinking from your thought ledger.

- Your conscious, disciplined movement toward Self-Realization is the trustee of your Y☯Universal Prosperity.

Refuse to hold a tin cup under the Niagara of Plenty.

- Money matters should be treated like a process, not an event – like a verb, and not a noun! In other words designing your money management plan based on long term static assumptions will become meaningless for financial health. (For example, see the fifth tip below).

- Having money is better than having no money, no savings account, long dry periods of unemployment, and too many lulls in prosperity – if only for comfort reasons.

- Here's the truth about the consumer price index (CPI). As of this writing, the government continues to calculate it incorrectly! The CPI may not reflect *your* cost of living because it's based on housing, education, and medical costs. Sooo, for retired people who own their homes, are finished with their own formal education and have paid for their children's education, and are covered by Medicare and supplemental medical insurance – these costs aren't relevant to their CPI costs of living expenses.

- Change the due dates for your bills. Sometimes you have enough money coming in to pay all of your monthly expenses, but your paychecks don't match up with the due dates for your bills. Many companies will negotiate reasonable payment due dates with you, if asked.

- Negotiate for a better deal with your cable company. Chances are that your wireless provider or your cable company are not going to call you up when they have lower rates available.

- Set modest savings goals. If the traditional financial advice of saving enough to cover 3 to 6 months' worth of expenses feels impossible, set a more modest goal that feels right for you. As a matter of fact, if you're employed by a firm, strive to maintain a minimum balance of 10% of your yearly income. If you're self-employed, go for 20% liquidity.

- When you think about it, having all of the money you'll ever need and plenty of affirmative prayers at hand are two of the best antiperspirants available.

- Stop sinking cash into things you don't use, such as that neglected membership to a high-end gym, phone land lines, civic clubs, on-line auto-pay memberships, etc.

- Track your cash flow. Some people might prefer to sit down once a week and do the math themselves by reviewing their online statements. No matter which tracking method you chose, the point is to scan your spending to make sure it lines up with your expectations.

- Pay your bills on time. Payment history is the #1 factor that goes into calculating your FICO score. For example, if you pay only the minimum monthly payment on a $2,400 balance (the amount the average consumer carries), it could take you 12 years to clear the card. In that time, you'll have paid an additional $1,978 in interest (calculated at a modest 14%). Another example, one late mortgage payment can knock 100 points off your credit score overnight, which will affect your ability to get the best interest rates on car loans, property, boats, appliances, etc.

- Limit or eliminate credit card debt. The so-called 'credit utilization ratio,' or the share of credit you use, is the second most important factor that goes into determining your FICO score. The best approach to keeping your credit card debt in check is to pay the card off in full each month in order to avoid interest charges. (We hear you laughing! We get it! This is not so easy to do these days!) If you can't afford to do that, keeping the balance to below 30% of the total available credit can still give lenders the impression that you're a responsible borrower. Pay the lowest card balance off first, and then add what you have been paying on the lowest card balance each month to the payment on the second to lowest card balance to pay it off. Repeat the process until you've paid all of the credit cards off!

- Invest in surge protectors for all of your expensive electronics products.

- If possible, get a 15 year mortgage. Also, apply for a no-closing cost refinance if you've been in your home for five years or more. That means you won't have to pay thousands of dollars in upfront closing costs for things like appraisals, underwriting and processing fees. Check with your mortgage company.
- The foundation for all of your future monetary prosperity is your current savings plus investments.

> *Invest in spiritual practices. Spiritual practices connect you with your true Divine Nature and fortify you from egocentric material appetites that'll end up costing you plenty of money. Plus, Spiritual practices keep you in a place of inner peace, and open you up to creative solutions, regardless of your financial situation.*

- A common rule of thumb is to spend no more than a third of your take-home pay on housing. That leaves room for other financial obligations, such as paying down debt, saving, and investing – and some money for fun.
- Live within your means. Discipline yourself to spend less than your take-home pay each month as a key Y☯Universal Prosperity practice. Failing to live within your means is the basic cause of virtually all financial difficulties.
- Be well – and reasonably – insured. Having health, homeowners, life, and vehicle insurance is not a sign of lack of faith; it is a sign of wisdom and understanding of "skin school."

- Eat at home more than you eat out. The occasional splurge or nice restaurant meal is fine, but the savings can really add up if you start cooking at home instead of eating out each day.

- We're reminded of many traditional religious pastors saying in their sermons: "You've got to give 'till it hurts!" We thought about that from our current spiritual perspective on the essence of giving and philanthropy, and intuited changing one of the words – Give 'till it **Hertz**! We wanted to take 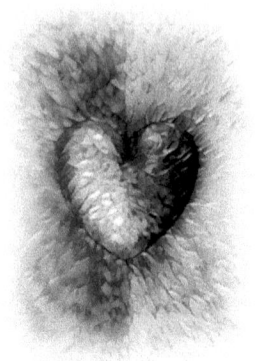 the 'pain and discomfort' out of giving and center a giving consciousness on the heart center which operates at **639 Hz** in the Solfeggio frequency.

- Invest in a fireproof safe. Keep at least one annually-inspected fire extinguisher for each floor of your house.

- Invest as much money as you can. Diversify your portfolio. You never want to have all of your money invested in just one type of stock or mutual fund, and especially not all in one business. Index funds and exchange-traded funds (ETFs) are an excellent investment because they provide broad market exposure, low operating expenses, and low portfolio turnover. Index funds are better than mutual funds because they avoid all of the usual costs associated with the frequent transactions touted by hungry 'money handlers.'

- Make your money make more money. Want to know how the rich keep getting richer? It's because money can grow while you sleep, provided you save some of it. Properly invested money earns more money over time! Don't sock all your cash away in a low-interest savings accounts. Invest in things that earn you a decent return.

- ☯ Take note that the stock market depends about as much on well-meaning stock market analysts as the weather depends on well-meaning meteorologists.

- ☯ Automate your retirement savings. Invest a set amount of your hard-earned monthly income in a tax-advantaged 401(k) or an IRA. When you get a raise or a little extra money, up your contribution!

- ☯ Generate more than one source of income. These days, more than one revenue stream helps. Make money on your hobbies, sell things online, work part time during seasonal job opportunities, write books and sell them, coach people on your expertise areas, etc. Diversity helps you avoid the 'ebb times.'

- ☯ To achieve the Y☯Universal riches you want, we encourage you to 'RSVP' your Divine Nature. That means:

    R: Realize that you're the human image of your G.O.D. Essence (your Global Omnipresent Divine Nature) actualizing *as* you.

    S: Screen your negative thoughts and emotions.

    V: Visualize successfully manifesting what you want.

    P: Pre-prayer your desires using affirmative prayer, followed up with spirited choices and actions.

- ☯ Enroll in classes on money management and investing basics. Diversify your classes. Don't take all of your classes from the same 'financial expert.'

- ☯ Set reminders for important money matters. If you don't trust yourself to remember to pay your quarterly taxes or periodically pull a credit report, set appointment reminders like you do for annual doctor's visits, paying vehicle or boat property taxes, vehicle maintenance, etc.

- Stock market prices are driven by emotion and the fickleness generated by fluctuations in the marketplace, and not by reality and common sense. Look for companies that have what's called 'a durable competitive advantage.' That means whether their stock price goes up or down, their operational strength and integrity will see their company outperform other stocks.

- Y☯Universalize your financial prosperity by localizing your thinking, being, and doing.

- Just so you know, although frugality seems to be an unfashionable word these days, it derives from the Latin *frux*, which means 'fruit or virture,' and from *frui*, which means 'enjoy or use well.' Soooo, frugality doesn't actually mean going without or being miserly, but enjoying what you have!

- Track your net worth. Your net worth (the difference between your assets and debt) is the big-picture number that shows where you stand financially. Stay apprised of the progress you're making toward your money matters goals. And remember (we know we already said this earlier, but it's worth repeating): Never confuse your net worth with your Self Worth!

- Set aside 60 seconds each day to check on your financial transactions. This 60-second peek helps identify glitches immediately, so you can track your money flow.

- Create a Money Management Vision Board. We're serious. Use this motivational technique to adopt better money management habits. You'll find that when you craft a vision board, it'll help remind you to stay on track with money matters. Adopt a money management mantra. For example, affirm: "I'm a wise, well, and happy financial manager of my money."

- When you purchase stocks, buy for the long haul.

- Gather several friends for regular money matters get-togethers. Friends with similar traits can pick up good habits from each other—and it applies to your money too!

- Never, ever cosign a loan. If the borrower – your friend, family member, significant other, whomever – is late on payments or misses payments, your credit score will take a hit. Lenders can come after you for the money, and it'll add financial liability you don't need. Plus, if the bank requires a cosigner at signing, the bank doesn't trust the person you've co-signed for to make the payments.

- People who aren't as financially rich as they'd like to be focus on their paycheck-to-paycheck net pay after taxes each week. Rich people focus on their net worth.

Out-of-body experiences are much more fulfilling than out-of-money experiences.

- Opt for mortgage payments below 28% of your monthly income. Why this target? During the housing boom, many people laid out unrealistic amounts of their gross income (sometimes 45% or higher) for their monthly mortgage payment, real estate taxes, and home owner's insurance. And everyone knows how that turned out (a foreclosure crisis). These days many banks have much tighter lending standards, meaning they may not lend to someone whose housing payments are liable to exceed the benchmark of about 28%. If you want a home that takes you over this limit, it won't be easy to get a loan. Typically, you'll need a minimum credit score of around 740 and a down payment of 10% or more.

- Evaluate purchases by cost per use. It may seem more financially responsible to buy a trendy $5 shirt than a $30 shirt – but only if you ignore the quality factor! When deciding if the latest tech toy, kitchen gadget, or apparel item is worth it, factor in how many times you'll use it or wear it. Here's the formula:

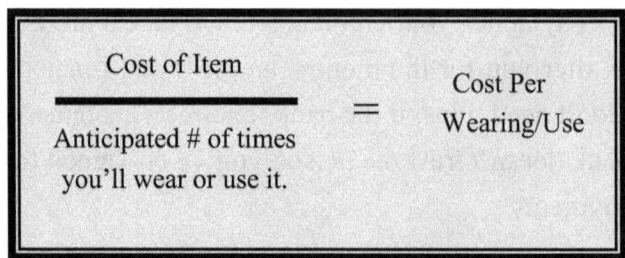

- Spend more on experiences than material things. Putting your money toward experiences, like a concert or a picnic in the park—instead of spending it on pricey material objects—gives you more long term happiness for your buck.

- Ditch the bank overdraft protection. It sounds nice, but it's actually a way for banks to tempt you to overspend, and then charge a fee for the privilege. Be disciplined – and watchful – with your banking habits.

- Review your credit report regularly. Keep a consistent and disciplined eye on your credit score.

- Investment opportunities are ones in which you vet the stock's reliability, soundness, and satisfactory return on investment. If you purchase a stock quickly because it's a 'great opportunity' without vetting it, you're simply speculating!

- Keep your savings out of your checking account. Here's a universal money matters truth: If you see you have extra money in your checking account, you'll spend it.

- Most people are way too busy earning a living nonchalantly to make any serious money.

- Open your savings account at a different bank or credit union than where you have your checking account. If you keep both your accounts at the same bank, it's easy – way too easy – way, way too easy – to transfer money from your savings to your checking. Did we say way too easy?

- As spiritual beings, we know money isn't the most important thing in life, but all things considered, it's pretty close to oxygen, perfect health, having the perfect soulmate, and experiencing nirvana on the 'gotta have it' list while living in skin school.

- Use your savings funds as a catalyst. If you have more than six months' savings in your emergency fund account (9 months if you're self-employed), and you have enough socked away for your short-term financial goals, invest the rest.

- Stick with low-cost index funds. The fees (expense ratios) you pay for your funds can eat into your returns. Even something as seemingly low as a 1% fee will cost you in the long run.

- Refrain from mindlessly playing the market. Take a look at your brokerage accounts every once in a while to make sure that your investment allocations still match your financial goals.

- Limit the number of credit cards you have. Select a low annual percentage rate (APR), which reduces the interest you'll have to repay. However, be aware of low introductory rates that increase after a period of time (usually six months). Also be aware of other charges (late payment fees, transaction fees, over the limit fees, etc.) that can add to the total cost of your overall charges. In order to maintain reasonable payments, keep your credit charges low (consider a limit of $1,000 or less).

- Opt out of interest rate increases. You can usually 'opt out' of any interest rate increase and continue to pay off your credit card balance at the current rate for up to five years.

- Avoid getting a big tax refund each year. This is a sign that you're probably having too much tax withheld from your paycheck. If this is the only way you're able to save, it's certainly better than nothing (assuming that you actually save and/or invest that money). Our concern is that it's not exactly the most effective way to save. Not only are you losing the ability to earn anything on that interest-free loan to Uncle Sam, but you also lose access to that money in the event of an emergency.

- Refinance high interest credit card debt. Consider the pros and cons of applying for a home equity loan or line of credit to pay off that credit card debt, because your interest rate could be much lower and also tax deductible. However, consider all the implications before making a decision (including taking it into meditation for an Intuitive Wisdom check).

- Balance your checkbook. These days, most people just rely on looking at their bank balance online every month or every couple of months. However, neglecting to see how much you're spending isn't a good practice. If you hold yourself accountable by monitoring your transactions, you'll avoid over-spending or overdrawing your accounts.

- Intoxicated with Higher Truth principles is a cool place to be. However, *intaxication* isn't a savvy place to be. It shows your naivete when it comes to IRS knowledge. *Intaxication* describes people's initial euphoria at getting an IRS refund until they realize the refund was their money in the first place.

- Invest in a few mutual funds. Just know that most mutual funds require a minimum initial investment amount, which is often $3,000 or more. There are, however, a few good mutual fund companies that have funds with low minimums of $100, $500, and $1,000, respectively.

- Save your loose change. We're not losing you with this suggestion are we? Loose change adds up! Use it to celebrate your astute money management by going out to your favorite restaurant or simply adding it to your savings account.

- Audit yourself. Follow your paper and/or digital trail. It pays to look at your spending on a quarterly basis to see if there are ways to cut back and put more money into savings or debt repayments.

- Save 90% of your windfalls and tax refunds. Every time you receive a windfall, such as a work bonus, inheritance, contest winnings, or tax refund, put a portion into an investment and/or savings account or pay on a credit card. If you receive a large windfall (i.e., multimillion dollar lottery win) leave your money in a money market fund for 6 months to a year and get the financial planning you need to make wise investments.

- Use only the ATMs at your bank or credit union. For example, using the ATM of another financial institution once a week might seem like no big deal, but if it's costing you $3 for each withdrawal, that's more than $150 over the course of a year. You can quickly see how much more you're dissing yourself if you use other banks or credit unions more than once a week.

- Use the 24 hour rule (aka, the sleep on it rule). These rules help avoid purchasing expensive or unnecessary items on impulse. In other words, separate needs from wants. Think over each nonessential purchase overnight, or for at least 24 hours. The ability to delay gratification goes a long way in helping you manage money. When you put off large purchases, rather than sacrificing more important essentials or putting a purchase on a credit card, you give yourself time to evaluate whether the purchase is necessary, and even more time to compare prices. This is particularly a good practice while you're shopping online, because you can add items to your cart or wish list and come back to them a day later.

- When it comes to 'now moments,' Carpe Diem is a good slogan. When it comes to receiving a daily allowance for any and all expenses you might incur each day, 'Carpe per Diem' is a cool catchphrase.

- As a general monetary practice, unsubscribe. Avoid temptation by unsubscribing from marketing emails to the stores where you tend to spend the most money. By law, each email is required to have an unsubscribe link, usually at the bottom of the email.

- Freeze your credit, literally. If you're having trouble controlling your credit card use, but don't want to cut up your credit card in case you need it at some point, freeze your credit card in a bag of water. Needing to thaw your card will force you to consider the purchase before you make it. You can *'freeze'* your digital spending too! Remove any cards you have "saved" at any sites online. This forces you to actually go find your card and type the card number and CSC code in order to purchase something.

- Designate one day a week as a 'no spend day.' Spare no amount of common sense to make that happen!

- Are you a Broadway show fan? Get unadvertised theater ticket discounts. Call, email, or tweet your nearby theater to ask about discount options that are often not well-advertised. Many theaters offer discounted seats for seniors, students, and young adults, such as 'pay-your-age' or 'pay-what-you-can' programs. Or they'll offer rush discounts of any unsold seats immediately before a show.

- Create a family spending limit on gifts. Discuss placing spending limits on gifts within your family and/or an agreement where you only purchase one gift for one person over the holidays. These limits tend to reduce expenditures and will be greatly appreciated by family members with less financial flexibility.

- Stick to water at restaurants. It's standard in the restaurant industry to double the cost of both alcoholic and non-alcoholic drinks (including bottled water) by three to five times. So an easy way to cut down on your restaurant spending without changing your habits too drastically is to skip the special beverages, alcoholic and non-alcoholic.

- It's easy to meet expenses! Everywhere you go, and anytime you go – they'll be there waiting for you.

- Go generic. Ask your physician if generic prescription drugs are a good option for you. Generic drugs can cost several hundred dollars less to purchase annually than brand-name drugs. And since physicians often don't know the costs you incur for a particular drug, you typically have to ask.

- Most people's fiscal issues stem from reconciling their gross over-consumptive habits with their net income.

- Comparison shop for prescription drugs. Don't just rely on the closest in-formulary drugstore, because the cost to you can vary significantly from pharmacy to pharmacy. Make sure to check out your local pharmacist, supermarkets, wholesale clubs, and mail-order pharmacies.
- Weatherproof your home. Caulk holes and cracks that let warm air escape in the winter and cold air escape in the summer. Your local hardware store has materials, and quite possibly useful advice, about inexpensively stopping unwanted energy loss.

> *Investing in your spiritual growth pays the best interest and yields the best dividends.*

- Keep the sun out. Close your blinds or curtains during hot summer days. Blocking the sunlight really does help to keep your house cooler.
- Check multiple sites for low airfares. Don't rely on a single airline search engine to show you all inexpensive fares. Some discount carriers prohibit their flights from being listed in third-party searches, so you need to check their websites separately.
- Earn cash back with rebate apps. There are a multitude of cash back and rebate apps out there today. Not only are they convenient to use, but you can also get money for the same purchase from multiple apps, helping you earn even more. Just be sure you perform your due diligence in checking out the safety, reliability, and success rate of the apps you are considering.

- Get schooled on the stock market, because every once in a while, it'll do something soooo reactionary and stupid that it'll take your money away.

- Don't get easily frightened by market fluctuations. Mainstream media can scare even the most disciplined investor. Be sure to focus on what you can control and be self-disciplined—be consistent and patient. Diversify your funds and ensure your investment portfolio is properly balanced. Also, do your best to avoid listening to and being affected by day-to-day marketplace noise.

- Have more than one checking account. If all your money is going into one account, it takes much more effort to keep track of everything. Make sure to have a minimum of two accounts—one for bills and one for discretionary spending. Figure out what your monthly bills are and divide that by the number of times you get paid in a month. If your bills are $4,000 a month and you get paid twice a month, then your direct deposit to the bills account would be a minimum of $2,000 each paycheck, and the remainder would go into your discretionary spending account.

- Purchase no-load rather than load mutual funds. Why? Because no-load mutual funds are funds in which shares are sold without a commission or sales charge. The absence of fees occurs because the shares are distributed directly by the investment company and not by commission-based brokers.

- Recognize that financial industry salespeople may not have your best monetary interests in mind. Some financial planners masquerade as honest fiduciaries and put their interests ahead of yours by recommending whatever investments pay them the highest commissions. Check the planner's CFP credentials.

- Many people have been programmed by their societies to have a poverty mentality. Don't be one of them! People who don't respect the nature of money don't have any. Don't be one of them! Money and political power are the chief currencies of the earth plane.

- If you're a good writer consider making one of your streams of income from '*infopreneuring*' (writing and selling books, blogs, articles, and other information products).

- A lot of people spend an awful lot of money on alcohol, illegal drugs, expensive bling, ridiculously-priced clothing, and over-priced luxury cars. The rest they simply squander.

- Consider exogenous vs endogenous implications. Exogenous factors include whether the stock market is going up or down, or whether the Federal Reserve will raise interest rates, or what the next global calamity will be. You have no control over these factors. However, compared to the impact that endogenous factors exert on your life and financial health, exogenous events are simply contextual. Endogenous factors include education, marriage, occupation, children, divorce, disability, layoffs, retirement, etc. These are the real money matters issues you need to address.

- Don't invest in a friend's 'you can't miss' investment tip or the proverbial financial 'home run.' Singles and doubles usually result in long-term wins.

- Use what you buy as often, as much and as long as humanly possible. What's the point in buying a new iPhone, video game system, golf clubs, TV, or pair of designer jeans if you're just going to pitch them when the next material enticement comes along?

- Asset allocation will ensure your uninterrupted liquidity. A portion of your portfolio needs to protect you from deflation and a portion must protect you from inflation. Bonds are the best way to guard against deflation, because, unlike stocks, they provide a fixed rate of interest over a long period of time. TIPS (Treasury Inflation-Protected Securities) are the best-in-breed inflation protectors, with leveraged loans and aggregate bonds coming in second and third. Bottom line, a properly balanced and diversified portfolio will protect you from both of these 'flations.'
- Keep all of your annual receipts. We recommend using Turbo Scan, an app that makes it easy to scan, save, and organize your receipts as you go.

> *Don't over-complicate things. Define your lifestyle and wrap your buying, saving, working, and investing around it.*

- Consider using FDIC-insured deposit accounts. Use a combination of certificates of deposit (CDs) which lock in your money for a fixed period of time at a rates that's typically higher than a regular savings account; IRAs; and securities like stocks and/or index funds.
- Avoid so called 'great deals' which end up grating on you.
- Don't underestimate the costs associated with ownership.
- Sound money management isn't so much about the amount of money you earn – it's more about your saving, investing, and spending habits.

- ☯ Spend money on healthy non-inflammatory foods and drinks. An inflammatory diet causes chronic and life-threatening illnesses. Consult a reputable nutritionist for life-changing dietary advice. You'll live healthily and longer and be able to enjoy the life you've worked soooo hard to achieve.

- ☯ Don't drink and spend, or lend, or bend the rules when it comes to money matters. If you do, it can be a sobering experience.

- ☯ About the time we think we can make ends meet, the quirky, fickled economy moves the ends.

- ☯ Take advantage of coupons. When you're trying to stick to a budget, always remember to check for coupons when you're shopping for essentials! Smartphone apps for couponing are worth putting a little research into, too. This makes good sen$e, right?

- ☯ Be very wary of investment gurus – by industry reputation or their own proselytizing – who say they can predict what's going to happen next in financial markets. Industry trends all come down to luck and luck comes down to a 50/50 coin toss.

- ☯ When you get to the point that you have more money than you can spend in your lifetime, we heartily applaud you. We also recommend three financial options: Increase your standard of living expenses on fun things (in other words, invest in good memories); gift $ away to your children, friends (get credible advice on transfer of wealth); and allocate a portion of it to charitable annuities and/or a donor-advised fund (DAF).

- ☯ Give yourself an annual money management physical.

- ☯ Remember to mail in rebate offers you've taken advantage of right after your purchase.

- Most people think money doesn't grow on trees. However, it does – on family trees! According to the Bureau of Engraving and Printing, US paper currency is made up of 75% cotton and 25% linen.

- Understand your over-all risk exposure. Stay away from brokers who recommend high risk stocks and illiquid real estate ventures. The risks in your investment portfolio should be congruent with other risks and responsibilities in your life. For example, how stable is your employment? How liquid are you? How much money matters knowledge do you have? What's your experience and emotional tolerance with risk? Does your current portfolio help insure you against both inflation and deflation? Here's the point: your risk tolerance is contextual – and you're the context!

Don't buy dumb stuff.

- Spiritual teachers talk about going with the flow instead of against it. Financial planners talk about going with the flow too. From their perspective it's called cash flow!
- Prefer debit cards over credit card debt.
- The key to unlimited prosperity is meeting limited human resources and circumstances with unlimited positivity.
- Follow the three Rules of sound money management: Rule #1: Cut expenses. Rule #2: *Absolivily positutely* live beneath your material yearnings. Rule #3: Never forget Rules 1 and 2.
- You don't have to be a money miser – just be wiser with your cash flow.

- Ever wonder why you don't hear about psychics or mentalists winning the state lottery?

- The best way to teach your children about the high cost of taxes is by eating a third of their pizza.

- It's good to have money and the things that money can buy. However, make sure you never lose the things that no amount of money can't buy.

- Follow J. Paul Getty's advice if you're playing the stock market: Buy when everyone else is selling and hold until everyone else is buying.

- Control your income and the spending that's usually associated with it, or your lack of income will very definitely control you.

- Only spend money on the things you value. It's as simple as that.

- Being a real stickler for the amount of money you spend each day usually doesn't last long for most people. Well, neither does flossing and brushing your teeth. That's why we recommend you're doing all three daily.

- Be under no illusion. The Stock Market is designed to shuffle money from the over-active to those who are perspiration-free patient.

- Remember, the more you allow your money to work for you, the less you'll need to work for your money.

- Your net worth is generally determined by what's left after your monetary mismanagement habits are subtracted from your good fiduciary habits.

- Empty pockets aren't the main issue when it comes to sound money management. It's the empty heads that create the empty pockets that's the real concern.

- Budget your money. A well-organized and well-monitored budget is telling your hard earned money where to go, instead of wondering what in the world happened to it.

- January is the absolute worst month to invest in highly speculative stocks. The other months are: February, March, April, May, June, July, August, September, October, November and December.

- Creating new debts isn't the way to pay off old ones.

- When you work on something that's only valued to pay you $65 an hour, it doesn't matter how hard you work – you'll still only make $65.

- How much do you need to earn on your savings and investment dollars to be able to retire at your current lifestyle and standard of living and have enough money to last your entire life expectancy?

- Be aware of frivolous spending on little expenses. A small leak dripping into the hold of a ship can eventually sink the ship. The same thing applies to your finances: wasting an amount as small as $3 each day will add up to a substantial loss of $1,095 by year's end. On the other hand, saving $3 each day adds up to $1,095 plus interest.

- Financial literacy is just as important as Truth principle literacy, lifestyle literacy, good relationship literacy, health and well-being literacy, diet and exercise literacy, meditation literacy, affirmative prayer literacy, etc.

- You are prosperous when you never have to do something you don't want to do just because of money, and never don't do something you want to do just because of money.

Be aware that claiming a tenfold return, a hundred-fold return, or simply some kind of a return – just because we give something to someone – isn't a consciousness of giving. It's a consciousness of entitlement.

- Paying yourself first can turn you into a millionaire over time thanks to the accumulation power of compound interest, even if you have just a modest income. You can read prosperity books, listen to 'Get Rich Quick' YouTubes, subscribe to financial newsletters, purchase motivational products, etc., but you'll never get the financial independence you want unless you PAY YOURSELF FIRST – before you pay any other bills. If you're in debt, pay yourself 5% as an automatic deduction until you reduce your debt. Then work up to paying yourself 10% or more as you liquidate your indebtedness.

- Sometimes you need to empty your pockets to fill your soul.

- Keep in mind that the funny thing about money is it not only changes hands – it changes people. The nice thing about it is it never clashes with anything you're wearing. The interesting thing about money is the more it's inflated, the less it can be stretched. The neat thing about it is you can't take it with you.

- For multiple streams of income to work consistently for you, you've got to stop your 'spending leaks.'

- As often as you can do it, refrain from paying retail for anything.

- From a wise perspective, the economics of spirituality means we have ready access to the omnipresent supply of Universal Substance. That means we have access to unlimited prosperity through the unmanifest Universal Bank of Abundance. The only deposits we have to make are faith, patience, and trust.

- A good money management plan involves seven important W's: What you do with it, why you do what you do with it, when you do it, where you do it, with whom you invest it, ways you use it, and the willpower employed to manage it.

- You won't achieve the monetary health you want by neglecting to invest wisely, and you most definitely won't establish healthy financial freedom on habitually borrowing money.
- Avoid all unnecessary debting!
- You can learn to master money, instead of being mastered by the lack of it!

> *Many people shun the path of their greatest joy, aliveness, and prosperity, thinking they can't make enough money from it.*

- Avoid taking your wealth out of circulation.
- Bonds are one of the best ways to guard against deflation, because, unlike stocks, they provide a fixed rate of interest over long periods of time.
- True fee-only fiduciary advisors (CFPs – Certified Financial Planners) charge an hourly rate or a fixed annual retainer. If you pay a transaction-based commission, the advisor is only a commissioned sales rep. Ask for Form ADV which shows he/she is a Registered Investment Advisor (RIA). If he/she can't – or won't – provide one, DO NOT HIRE HIM/HER as your financial planner!

Spiritual Practice: 30-Day Y☯Universal Prosperity Challenge

You can realize and demonstrate abundant prosperity in your life, by practicing the Y☯Universal Prosperity Principles. Take time to review them.

Y☯ Universal Prosperity: the soul growth we attain when we align our Human Nature with our Divine Nature, so we actualize Divine Health, Happiness, Inner Peace, and Financial Security. The secret to mastering the art of living prosperously is to make your life a Spiritual Practice which expands your Prosperity Consciousness, and provides an opportunity to put the Principles into action!

This 30-day Prosperity Plan is designed to help you experience success! Research supports the fact that it takes about 30 days for your consciousness to realize higher Truths at the conscious level of mind. Therefore, we recommend a commitment to faithfully follow this program for 30 days.

This Prosperity Plan combines two areas of focus:
- Strengthening your awareness of the incredible number of ways prosperity flows into your life;

- Creating a Spiritual Practice of consciously setting aside a portion of everything that flows in, committing to return it to Source through channels which have blessed your spiritual growth, thus claiming your status as one who believes in the Giving & Receiving Cycle.

Here's what you need to do to get started:

- *Prepare a special calendar, marking the day you begin your 30-day Prosperity Plan.* Count out 30 days from that start date, to signify the end of your first 30-days. (We believe you will be so amazed with the results that you will want to continue with this practice!) Remember, if you need to start over, just identify your next 30-day period. (No guilt!)
- *Decide on a percentage of your income to use for this 30-day plan.* We recommend a percentage that feels like a bit of a stretch for you, but not unrealistic. Most people feel comfortable choosing something between 3% and 10% — but if you are already regularly giving 10% or more of your income to channels of your spiritual enrichment, then we suggest you up it by at least 3%.
- *Prepare a business-size or larger envelope.* On the front write these words:
  This is my Spiritual Prosperity Practice Envelope. Every day I will deposit ____% of all my income for the day, both expected and unexpected.
- *Create a Prosperity Journal.* Set aside some kind of notebook or journal strictly to use with this Prosperity Plan. Divide it into three sections:

    Part 1: Notes from my Daily Meditation Practice
    Part 2: Recognition of Expected and Unexpected Income
    Part 3: Recording of Daily Spiritual Giving Practice, and notes to track any surprises, life changes, and serendipities!

The 30-Day Prosperity Challenge Process:

- Set aside **30 minutes each day** to commit to the Prosperity Consciousness Expansion Process.

- Spend 5 minutes allowing yourself to get centered and peaceful. Release all worries, fears, and concerns and focus on your breath, becoming very aware of your inhalation (thinking the words "I am One …") and exhalation ("and at peace.")

- Focus your attention on the affirmation designated for that day (listed below). Repeat it aloud a minimum of three times, and write it three times in your journal. Then close your eyes and meditate on the affirmation for 10 minutes or longer.

- Once you come out of your meditation, capture any thoughts you have in your Prosperity Journal. Thoughts might include people to forgive, things or beliefs to release, fears to face and act through, service for you to provide, and Divine ideas to attract prosperity.

- At the end of each day, determine the appropriate amount for your Spiritual Giving Practice, based on income (both expected and unexpected), applying the percentage you selected. Using your Spiritual Prosperity Practice Envelope, prayerfully and joyfully deposit the appropriate amount into the envelope, saying again the affirmation for the day. Record your deposit in your Journal, and check off the day on your calendar to celebrate your successful accomplishment of the Prosperity Plan.

- At the end of each week, choose one or more channels contributing to your spiritual enrichment and make donations to sources of your spiritual enrichment (using the money you have placed in your envelope) as your **Prosperity Celebration** for the week. Repeat all the affirmations you have used throughout the week, with enthusiasm and joy. Honor your generosity of spirit as you give.

- **Share your experiences with a "Prosperity Partner" (someone willing to go through this challenge with you).** This reinforces your commitment to continue with the Challenge — and it contributes to your Prosperity Experience. (One big secret of Prosperity consciousness is a Consciousness of Giving, and by sharing your experiences and giving feedback to others, you are priming the Prosperity Pump!) If you can't find a partner, consider us as supporting you — and email us to keep us posted on your progress!

Affirmations:

We have created five different affirmations. Use one each day, which results in working with each of them six times during the 30-day process. Feel free to adapt these slightly to include whatever terms resonate with you, such as Divine Spirit, Field of Infinite Potential, The One, God, etc.

> **#1:** My Consciousness is greater than any fear I feel! I am one with the instant, constant, inexhaustible Source of my abundant, manifested supply.
> **(Days 1, 6, 11, 16, 21, 26)**
>
> **#2:** I release everyone who has injured or harmed me in any way, and affirm the highest and best for each person. I also forgive myself for any choices I have made that were not for my highest good. My way is now clear and free for abundant flow in unexpected and amazing ways.
> **(Days 2, 7, 12, 17, 22, 27)**

#3: I let go of anything that is no longer serving me, and open sacred space for my abundant good to manifest. I give and receive joyfully, knowing there is always plenty! I am meant to prosper! I am rich, healthy, happy, and at peace in all areas of my life.
(Days 3, 8, 13, 18, 23, 28)

#4: Only thoughts of health, plenty, and joy fill my mind. I step forward in faith, knowing the Infinite Field of Potential is open to me, and I am richly blessed. I deserve to be prosperous, and money flows to me easily and effortlessly!
(Days 4, 9, 14, 19, 24, 29)

#5: Nothing stands in my way of Divine Abundance! I sizzle with zeal and enthusiasm, living in a spirit of generosity and love, knowing that abundant resources are manifesting with speed, ease, comfort, and joy! I am grateful!
(Days 5, 10, 15, 20, 25, 30)

Part 3:

Understanding Your Human and Divine Natures to Accelerate Your Y☯Universal Prosperity

Your Y☯Universe includes the phenomenal duet of two Natures:

- **Human Nature**: the flesh and blood you that's going through your current skin school experience. It includes both your waking consciousness and your subconsciousness, which is the composite consciousness of all of your reincarnational and incarnational selves. (It also includes concurrent parallel universe selves that are warehoused (embedded) in your current subconsciousness, which is filled with your past life tendencies and patterns, and current newly formed subconscious tendencies and patterns – but that's another whole book!)
- **Divine Nature**: your timeless Universal, Transcendental, Eternal Spiritual Nature that is underwritten by your *Soul Signature*, which is your personalized Life Force and Personal Identity in the Cosmos, actualizing through your Super-Consciousness (your Upper Room).

Y☯Universal Prosperity is all about bringing these two Natures into alignment, by learning how to manage the various polarities associated with both our skin school experiences and our eternal beingness in other dimensions of being, so we can align our Human Nature with our Divine Nature. In other words, Y☯Universal Prosperity is polarities management during our skin school experience. A few examples of the polarities in your Y☯Universe are:

- the human you and the Divine you,
- the finite you and the infinite you,
- the thoughtful you and the emotional you,
- the unenlightened egocentric you and the fully enlightened Self-Centric You,

- the physical you and the ethereal you,
- the yang you and the yin you,
- the spiritual you and the religious you,
- the limited you and the limitless you,
- the materialistic you and the philanthropic you,
- the meditative you and the active you,
- the dogmatic you and the enlightened thinker you,
- the pessimistic you and the optimistic you,
- the earthly you and the cosmic you,
- the exploring you and the practical you, and so on.

Included in this section, you'll discover many practical insights, guidance, and evidence-based spiritual techniques for harmonizing your Y☯Universe. For example, breathe in and then breathe out. Inhale and now exhale. If you neglect to consistently do this, any concerns about your eventual enlightenment, or the best mantra or affirmative prayer technique to use, or the right guru or spiritual teacher to examine, or which password to use for your online banking will be the least of your concerns. Breathing is essential, whether you do it consciously or allow it to happen on its own! There is both science and practicality involved in breathing; in the same way, you'll see that our MetaSpiritual approach is both scientific and practical. It all begins with understanding your Human and your Divine Natures, so you can more easily bring them into alignment … and keep them there!

Our Human Nature Explored

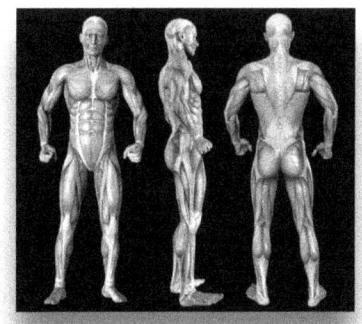

Inside of your physical Y☯Universe, in the microcosm of your inner being, there are the subtle vibrations of a molecular world. You're composed of communes, colonies, cities, and continents of trillions of cells in action. Your body is filled with cellular life. You're composed of hydrogen atoms and subatomic particles like quarks, leptons, and gluons that were present at the 'big bang' that birthed our universe. Quantum physicists tell us that you're literally stardust as a physical being. Subatomic parts of you are 12.5 to 13 billion years old. Other parts of you are a billionth of a second old. At a molecular and cellular level, your physical Y☯Universe (your human body) is a quantum container that's the outer expression of your Superconsciousness which created it.

We're convinced that in order to fully understand what it means to be a human being, we must understand something about the 'realness' of our human nature. And in order to grasp what it means to truly be human ,we've got to understand the underlying dynamics of our Human Nature, which are influenced by not only our own subconscious patterns and past life tendencies, but the collective subconscious patterns of the entire human race.

Sooooo, we're going to lead off with the following awareness: In the early days of humankind's appearance on earth, we chose to gravitate toward the banks of rivers to stimulate our commerce, livelihood, and sense of community. As of this writing, humankind is headed toward living along a single global river of algorithm-driven data and information that will revolutionize and redefine our worldwide commerce, characterize our collective livelihood, and determine our international sense of community. This digitized globalization can lead to our collective oneness or our extinction as a species. Here's what a few enlightened people say about being human:

> *Religious teachers have told us that it is the soul that makes us human. However, I believe it is when we are most human that we have the greatest access to the soul.* (Thomas Moore, Irish poet)

> *When I say that human nature is gentleness, it's not 100% so. Every human being has that nature, but there are many people acting against their nature, being false.* (14th Dalai Lama, Tibetan Buddhist monk)

> *We must see in every person a universe with its own secrets and its own treasures.* (Elie Wiesel, American Jewish writer and Nobel Laureate)

> *There's a very remarkable inclination in human nature to bestow on external objects the same emotions which it observes in itself.* (David Hume, Scottish philosopher)

> *I think it says something about human nature that the only form of life we've created so far is purely destructive. We've created life in our own image.* (Stephen Hawking, English theoretical physicist)

> *No matter how happy anyone is with their choices, It's human nature to wonder about the path not taken.* (Jen Lancaster, American author)

Here's how various scientific disciplines describe Human Nature. **Feel free to skip over this section if science isn't your cup of tea!** We just found it interesting to capture a snippet of how the different disciplines view our Human Nature, because the way you view it has a dramatic impact on how you study it and work to understand it!

- ***Paleoanthropologists*** identify the category of the human with the species *Homo sapiens*, while some restrict it to the subspecies *Homo sapiens sapiens,* and a few take it to encompass the entire hominin lineage.
- ***Geneticists*** tell us that what it means to be human depends on heredity, instincts, genes, reflexes, associations, history, formative experience, cultural influences, division of labor, development, and imprinting. All of these things characterize human beings. No account of human nature would be complete without all of them. Ongoing fossil discoveries confirm that the first 4 million years or so of human evolutionary history took place exclusively on the African continent. It's there that the search continues for fossils at or near the branching point of the chimpanzee and human lineages from our last common ancestor. DNA also shows that our species and chimpanzees diverged from a common ancestor species that lived between 8 and 6 million years ago.
- ***Anthropologists*** explain that human biology is and always will be a dynamic interaction of processing, not hard-wiring. Human capacities aren't genetically specified, but emerge within processes of ontogenetic development. They tell us that all modern humans evolved from an oasis called the Makgadikgadi-Okavango wetland in Botswana. There's no way of describing what human beings are, independently of the manifold historical and environmental circumstances in which they grow up and live out their lives. That means seeing biology and culture as definitively defining what it means to be human isn't just clumsily imprecise; it's the single major stumbling block that's prevented us from

moving towards an understanding of our human selves, and of our place in the living world.
- ***Embryologists*** say we're uniquely human from the moment that egg and sperm fuse at fertilization. A 'human program' begins before the brain even begins to form. There's absolutely no question whatsoever that the immediate product of fertilization is a newly existing human being. A human zygote *is* a human being. It's *not* a 'potential' or a 'possible' human being. It's an actual human being with the potential to grow bigger and mature. Every moment of development blends into the next succeeding moment. But, even common sense tells us that this so-called development does not cease at birth. It continues until death. At any point in time, during the continuum of life, there exists a whole, integrated human being.
- According to ***neuroscientists***, the critical unique factors that make us uniquely human are: complex language, superior intellect, creativity, a religious and scientific impulse, and our social and technological orientations. We have a recorded history of moral behavior, economics, politics, and social institutions. We're probably uniquely suited in our ability to investigate the future, imagine outcomes, and display images in our minds.
- According to ***evolutionists***, thousands of years ago interaction with the harsh world progressively transformed ape-like creatures into progressively more human-like creatures and finally into full-fledged humans. However, human beings aren't just a sum of parts that finally crossed a line and became human. We're composed of hydrogen atoms and subatomic particles like quarks, leptons, and gluons that were present at the 'big bang' that created our universe. The nitrogen in our DNA came from the interiors of collapsing

stars. The carbon dioxide we exhale on every breath came from planetary nebulas. Our connection to nature and to the earth (Gaia) as a whole is innate and symbiotic. We are the Life Force quantized and particularized as us. We are spiritual beings made out of star stuff in our quantum (physical) form!

- According to the ***religious faithful***, we humans didn't evolve from apes at all, but were created in the image of an anthropomorphic God (*imago dei*) who is believed to have had human qualities, who loved his creation beginning with the 'first human couple' into whom he breathed life.
- Human behavior is algorithmically transferable. ***Robotics scientists*** are asking when robots' behavior will become indistinguishable from human behavior. Is our fetishization of technology making us behave in a more robotic way?
- ***Transhumanists*** believe that the human race can evolve beyond its current physical and mental limitations, especially by means of science and technology. A transhuman is a person who *is* merely human, but has gone beyond the "maximum attainable capacities" by any current human being … in other words, a superbeing by today's standards. It would mean people who, through genetic manipulation, the use of stem cells, or other bio-intervention, have had their ability to remain healthy and active extended beyond what we would consider normal. Their cognitive powers (memory, deductive thought and other intellectual capabilities, as well as their artistic and creative powers) would far outstrip humans who weren't 'transhumanized.'
- ***Posthumanists*** claim we could achieve being people who have their bodies upgraded using advanced nanotechnologies such as genetic engineering, psychopharmacology, anti-aging therapies, neural interfaces, memory enhancing drugs, wearable computers, and advanced cognitive techniques. The

human species is still young on this planet (we've only been around 6 million years – the Plesiadapiformes likely contain the ancestor species of all primates, including us humans. However, the Proconsul Africanus, of 23 million years ago, is a possible ancestor of both great and lessor apes, including us humans), and it's possible that we've only seen little of what's possible for us to become more human than we are already.

- According to our **MetaSpiritual perspective**, we 'rent' a physical vehicle, which turns out to be a hybrid of the Tree of the Knowledge of Good and Error and the Tree of Life, so we can consciously continue an uninterrupted soul journey toward our complete and full Self-Realization. This physical vehicle is our psycho-somatic spacesuit.

As we further explore our Human Nature, here are some interesting, generalized particulars that define our human physical characteristics according to scientists:

- Upright posture
- Clothing (We constantly invent clothing and wear it for different purposes)
- Extraordinary brain functions and brain power that allow us to invent and use incredible technologies. While humans have the largest brains proportional to body weight of all animals, we don't have the biggest brains. That distinction belongs to sperm whales with 17-pound brains.
- Hand dexterity (Other animals have opposable thumbs).
- The use of fire, and creating different forms of fire. (natural, electrical, chemical and biochemical, ionizing radiation [x-rays, gamma, etc.], non-ionizing [microwave, incandescent light bulbs, electric heaters, etc.], nuclear).

- Blushing (we're the only species known to blush) and wear cosmetics
- Long childhood care (altricial in nature)

Some other characteristics about being human:
- The biggest contributors to the chemical value of our body appear to be the *alkali metals* – lithium, sodium, potassium, rubidium and caesium. Potassium appears to be the single most 'valuable' element in our body. So, keep adding bananas to your diet.
- When we total the monetary value of the elements in our bodies and the value of the average person's skin, we arrive at a net worth of $4.50!
- Water is the most abundant chemical compound in our cells, accounting for 65% to 90% of each cell. It's also present between cells.
- Oxygen is the most abundant element in the human body, accounting for 65% of our body mass.
- Nerve impulses to and from the brain travel as fast as 170 miles per hour.
- Our body is estimated to have 60,000 miles of blood vessels.
- The surface area of a human lung is equal to a tennis court.
- Sneezes regularly exceed 100 mph and coughs clock in at about 60 mph.
- The strongest muscle in the human body is the tongue. We're not going to say anything more about that physiological finding. We know what you're thinking. Don't even go there!
- It's not possible to intentionally tickle yourself.
- 98.8% of our DNA is known as Junk DNA. Junk DNA is genomic DNA that doesn't encode proteins, and whose function isn't well understood.

- We have super abilities like: Absolute pitch, echolocation, pica (eating metal), X-ray vision, hyperthymesia (ability which allows people to pinpoint the smallest autobiographical details), speak 6,500 different languages, lift cars off of people, etc.
- We have the ability to remiss from Stage 4 illnesses.
- We have the ability to explore our religious and spiritual dimensions to come up with our concept of Reality, whether it's an anthropomorphic creator god or a universal Beingness that doesn't have human qualities.

What About Our Subconscious?

Our Human Nature also warehouses the composite consciousness of all of our reincarnational and incarnational selves, and concurrent parallel universe selves which underwrite our current physicality. During our current skin school experience, it serves as our subconsciousness.

The function of our subconsciousness, which psychologists call our subconscious mind, is to store and retrieve data. Its job is to ensure that we respond exactly the way we've programmed ourselves through many physical lifetimes. Our subconscious mind makes everything we think, say and do fit a pattern consistent with our accumulated self-concept.

Our subconsciousness sounds an awful lot like an Internet 'filter bubble,' where users become separated from information that may disagree with their current viewpoints, effectively isolating them in their own pre-established cultural and ideological bubbles. The term comes from the search engines on the Internet, which use algorithms of an Internet user's past browsing and search history (i.e., interest in topics by clicking links, viewing friends, putting

YouTubes and movies in their queue, reading news stories, purchasing certain products on line, and so on). The search engine then selects items to show the user that correlate with their cumulative past history, thereby effectively weeding out information outside the current level of interest and understanding, and limiting what the user is exposed to.

Using the 'filter bubble' analogy as a metaphor for our subconsciousness, think about the implications of your current thinking in general, and for your current spiritual or religious beliefs in particular. The function of your subconscious mind (your own personal filter bubble) is to store and retrieve data related to you. Its job is to ensure that you respond exactly the way you're programmed by others as well as yourself. Your subconscious mind makes everything you think, say, and do fit a pattern consistent with your self-preservation and self-concept.

Just so we're clear, your 'subconscious filter bubble' stores all of your memories and experiences in the form of images and symbols during your human incarnations as well as your other dimensional incarnations. Emotions are the language of your subconscious mind and everything you see, in 'real life' or in a dream is considered real by the subconscious mind.

Neuroscientists show that most of our decisions, actions, emotions and behavior depend on the 95% of brain activity that's beyond our conscious awareness, which means that 95% of our thinking and behavior is influenced by the composite programming in our subconscious mind.

It's extremely important to understand this fact: in order to make a deep long-term change in the composite patterns we've established, our current ideas, perceptions, worldviews, customs, and beliefs must change the paradigms we've stored in our subconscious mind. And we have the power to do just that when we 'up our consciousness' to a super-conscious level.

It involves our willingness to do what we call "Question Unquestioned Answers." This means consciously challenging our own confirmation biases and beliefs, to play with ideas and understandings, and allow ourselves to replace outdated ideas that no longer work for us with something different, deeper, more powerful. Here's a process we use to question our unquestioned answers on a regular basis:

Questioning Unquestioned Answers
Spiritual Practice

- What is the Unquestioned Answer/Belief?
- How am I using this Belief now?
- If I believe this, what are the implications?
- How do I explain situations that conflict with my belief?
- What concerns or issues do I have about changing this belief?
- Through meditation and questioning, what new ideas are emerging about this belief?
- How might I tweak/rephrase/change this belief?

© 2020 Revs. Bil & Cher Holton, TheGlobalCenterForSpiritualAwakening.com (adapted from Questioning Unquestioned Answers Retreat)

Our Divine Nature Explored

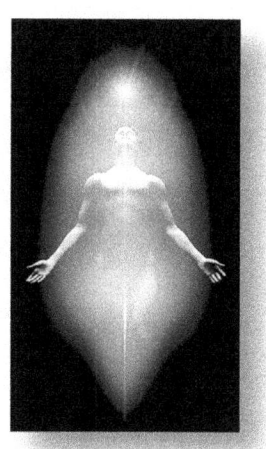

The second Nature of your Y☉Universal duet is your Divine Nature. It's also known as your Higher Self, your Super Self, the Extraordinary You, the Upper Room. It's the least understood and least accessed aspect of our dual Natures, mainly because it hasn't been acknowledged or taught in mainstream religion, science, or education.

Its domain is the spiritual realm. It's the Y☉Universal You that's the human expression of the Omnipresent Universal Reality at the point of you! It's the Divine You that's not only beyond the limitations of the physical world, but also beyond the limitations of other dimensions of being in which you've found yourself from time to time.

Your Higher Self doesn't distinguish between good or bad, right or wrong, happy or sad – not because it's unable to, but because it has no need to. It's the You that knows only Y☉Universal Prosperity. It's the Divine Singularity that gave birth to your Divine Nature and underwrites all that is.

Your Divine Nature knows that the physical, outside world you experience is 'frozen' Spirit. It knows that your circumstances, whether wanted or unwanted, are simply a reflection of your inner world, which itself is a product of the Y☉Universal You. It knows that your Divine Nature is the spiritual mirror that your Higher Consciousness has produced. Your Superconsciousness, the Upper Room, is omnipotent, omnipresent, omniscient, and omni-active.

It's Pure Energy vibrating at different frequencies. Your Superconsciousness isn't something you need to acquire or look for outside of yourself. You already possess it. All you need to do is become consciously aware of it and learn to access it.

Unfortunately, most people are totally unaware they have a superconscious aspect. Moreover, most people sleepwalk through life, unwittingly allowing all the messages they're bombarded with to be recorded in their subconsciousness. This ultimately leaves their lives highly influenced by their subconscious programming.

All of the things that you've learned about the universe are stored in your Y☯Universal Self. All of this information and knowledge is handled by your Divine Nature.

Decide, in this now moment, to place your conscious mind on guard at the door of your subconscious mind. Decide to allow only empowering, positive, nurturing, life-affirming messages to pass through that door. Decide to hand over the direction of your conscious mind to your Divine Nature, which is the epicenter for your super-consciousness. In so doing so, you'll raise your soul vibration to a state of Y☯Universal Prosperity.

Learn to be the unshakable witness to your old patterns and behaviors, knowing that they're simply replaceable. They're only programs of negative karma that have found a nesting place in your subconsciousness.

Know that through disciplined use of powerful spiritual practices, these old patterns will in time be replaced by new empowering thoughts, choices, behaviors, and beliefs. By allowing your dual Natures to come into alignment, you'll create the Y☯Universal Prosperity you need to attain full and complete Self-Realization.

Here's what other enlightened people have said about their Divine Nature:

My Me is GOD. (Catherine of Genoa, in 1501 CE)

GOD is a verb, not a noun. (Buckminster Fuller, in 1970 CE)

I don't believe in an anthropomorphic GOD... I believe in a Universal Divine Principle, the root of ALL from which all proceeds ... The only GOD we must recognize and pray to is that spirit of GOD of which our body is the temple, and in which It dwells. (Helena Blavatsky, Theosophical Society co-founder)

GOD is the Creator, the ruler of the universe. GOD is not a person, but Principle. (Charles Fillmore, The Unity Movement's co-founder).

An authoritarian god is associated with the oldest, most primitive amygdala structures of the brain, whereas a unitive or mystical GOD is experienced through the most recently evolved neuroplasticity of the brain. (Andrew Newberg, neuroscientist)

We are the activity of GOD expressing or pressing out into visibility as us. (Eric Butterworth, Unity minister)

GOD and I, we are one. By the living GOD, it is true that there is no distinction. (Meister Eckhart, mystic)

When the veil of the ego's ignorance was lifted, I understood that my true, underlying identity is, and has always been, the One All-Pervading Consciousness that is the Source and substratum of all that exists. (Swami Marie Abhayananda)

If you advance confidently in the direction of your dreams, and endeavor to live the life which you have imagined, you will meet with a success unexpected in common hours. You'll put some things behind and pass an invisible boundary; new, universal and more liberal laws will begin to establish themselves around and within you – Old laws will be expanded and interpreted in your favor in a more liberal sense; and you will live with license of a higher order of things. [Henry David Thoreau-(paraphrased)]

When the mystery of the oneness of the soul and the Divine is revealed to you, you will understand that you are not other than GOD. (Ibn Arabi, Sufi mystic)

In the beginning, there was existence alone – One Self! Out of Itself, It entered into creation. All that exists is this Self. And we are that Self. (Daniel Matt, Kabbalah scholar)

We'd like to mention what we believe to be our, yours, everyone's Divine Genealogy. Paleontologists, evolutionary anthropologists and paleoanthropologists, have classified us in some very interesting classifications. You've no doubt heard of these: Homo Sapiens, Homo Sapiens Sapiens, Homo Georgicus, Homo Ergaster, Homo Erectus, Homo Habilis, etc.

Our Spiritual Genealogy has only three classifications which we believe are higher spiritual level classifications than the other classifications. The three classifications we propose are based on a ton of higher consciousness research that describe the journey toward our Y☯Universal Selfhood. MetaSpiritually speaking, our Spiritual Genealogy is:

- **Homo Deus Unaware:** When we're born into skin school or another dimension of beingness, we're unaware of our Y☯Universal Consciousness Status.
- **Homo Deus Awakening**[1]**:** We spend many lifetimes trying to establish the Y☯Universal harmony we need to attain enlightenment and Self-Realization.
- **Homo Deus Actualized**[2]**:** We master the art of living in skin school and in whatever dimension of beingness we find ourselves when we achieve the endless and complete Y☯Universal Prosperity it takes to become fully Self-Realized.

[1] Chpt 15 in Bil's metaphysical interp of the *Book of Revelation* describes in detail what our Homo Deus Awakening status looks like.

[2] Chpt 20 in Bil's metaphysical interp of the *Book of Revelation* outlines our fully enlightened Homo Deus Actualized status).

The Power of OM

MetaSpiritually, the OM sound literally underwrites everything, manifests everything, and energizes everything. It immaculately conceives the manifest from the unmanifest, matter from Spirit, something from nothing!

Here's what's interesting about our dual *Y☯Universal Self* using the OM symbol to explain it. The OM symbol consists of three curves, one semicircle, and a dot::

- The large lower curve symbolizes our Human Nature (current skin school personality) which is influenced by our 30+ physical senses and our skin school subconsciousness.
- The upper curve explicitly refers to our Divine Nature (Superconsciousness) which can lead us to the realization of our highest state of bliss.
- The middle curve symbolizes our subconscious nature (the composite consciousness and sentient experience of all of our incarnations and reincarnations).
- The semicircle symbolizes our Self-Realization potential. It's open at the top, and doesn't touch the dot. This means that this highest state of bliss isn't affected by maya which only affects the manifested universe.
- The dot signifies the blissful state of consciousness when we become fully Self-Realized and is the ultimate aim of all of our spiritual growth.

We verbalize the OM sound three times as we move into a meditation, to ground us in the power of this sound. It is also electrifying to verbalize OM three times before you state an affirmation. And here's a little tidbit about us! We borrowed the Jewish custom of placing a mezuzah at our doorway to spiritually elevate the entry to and exit from our home. We have hung a plaque with the OM symbol next to our doorway, and touch it as we enter and exit.

Part 4:
Our Seven Core Abilities that will help you accelerate your Y☯Universal Prosperity

Authentegrity
Intuitive Wisdom
Inner Strength
Optimistic Spirit
Questioning Unquestioned Answers
Self-Reliance
Giving Consciousness

We can categorically tell you from our personal experience and from the last fifty years of human potential research we've compiled that when your "ordinary self" (the everyday you) is aligned with your Core Essence (your Divine Nature, your Higher Nature, the Extraordinary You), you can meet any human challenge with grace and poise. You can achieve things you thought were impossible. You can most assuredly find the happiness, joy, prosperity, and sense of inner peace you seek.

People who have discovered their true self, their Core Essence, have seven things in common, which we call your Seven Core Abilities. We have assigned each Core Ability a color, which reflects the essence of the ability.

1. Authentegrity (Red)
2. Intuitive Wisdom (Yellow)
3. Inner Strength (Russet Brown)
4. Optimistic Spirit (Orange)
5. Questioning Unquestioned Answers (Deep Blue)
6. Self-Reliance (Purple)
7. Giving Consciousness (Green)

Let's do a quick dive into each of these Core Abilities so you have a basic understanding of what each one offers, recognizing that there is much more to learn as you grow in your ability to call on these Core Abilities to master the art of living in skin school!

Authentegrity

A**uthentegrity** is a mash-up word combining two valuable qualities: Authenticity and Integrity. It is your ability to align your thoughts, words, and actions with the authentic values you embrace. It means being true, genuine, and real —no matter what the situation or results – and doing what you say you'll do.

The Color Red: Red is the color of energy and passion. It signifies your life force, and represents determination and conviction. Red is the color of Authentegrity because when you operate from that place of alignment, you live from conviction and intention, and are able to embrace life with energy and passion, knowing you are being true to the Extraordinary You!

Using the color RED to strengthen your Core Ability of Authentegrity: If you want to strengthen your awareness of your Authentegrity, make red your color of focus. Choose to wear something red as part of your wardrobe; eat foods that are red in color (apples, cherries, kidney beans, tomatoes, strawberries, red peppers, salsa, red-velvet cake, etc.); place items that are red in your environment (red flowers, a red stone, pictures with red as a dominant color); use red ink or markers when you write.

While this may feel a little silly at first, allow yourself to give it a try without judgment. Become aware of how much stronger you feel in terms of living in alignment with your values, and how you are experiencing Authentegrity in your life.

A Sampling of Hors d'Oeuvres Related to Authentegrity

- ☯ Recognize that people who are interested in cutting edge spirituality know that genuine, unpretentious Authentegrity is real and photoshopped integrity is fakery.

- ☯ Have absolutely zero doubt that no price is too high for the privilege of owning your Authenticity, no matter what happens to you in skin school.

- ☯ Know that Authentegrity is the lasting marriage between authenticity and integrity. You can look forward to celebrating their timeless anniversary in you as you attain more and more Y☯Universal Prosperity.

- ☯ Notice that when you find just the right mix of open communication and respectful privacy, distance and closeness, your full disclosure, sincerity, and confidentiality exemplify how authentic people approach relationships.

- ☯ Be aware that people who are on the path toward Y☯Universal Prosperity seem to epitomize a high degree of Authentegrity … and avoid majoring in minor things.

- Acquire a thirst for Authentegrity. It'll keep you from being ahead of yourself, beside yourself, and behind yourself as you walk the Y☯Universal Path on divinely-attuned feet.

> *Carefully wrap your promises around timeless Truth principles.*

- Know that Y☯Universally conscious people specialize in aligning their Human Nature with their Divine Nature.

- Understand that between stimulus and response there's an inner space, and in that space is your power to choose how you'll respond. In neurology, this one-third-of-a-second 'space' is called the *Bereitschafts Potential*. It's a prewired neurological moment that defines how aligned you are with your Authentegrity.

- Realize that in today's highly complex global community, you'll be constantly invited to lean toward your Y☯Universal Prosperity.

- Note that Authentegrity is unreservedly, unhesitatingly, and unapologetically accessing and then expressing the best parts of yourself.

- Recognize that the only person who can author your own Authentegrity is you.

- Distance yourself from people who grow more artificial by the minute.

- Note that straying away from the lamppost of Authentegrity keeps you in the dark.

- Don't settle for a relationship, business, or organization that wants to sabotage your being true to yourself, or settle for a cardboard cutout image of yourself that retails a paper thin you.

- Instead of looking outside to validate yourself, go inside to your innermost being. That's where the Extraordinary YOU lives. That's the seat of your Y☯Universal Prosperity.

- Let who you really are, what you really are, where you are currently, and when you are by right of consciousness emanate out of everything you think, say, decide, and do.

- Understand that Authentegrity epitomizes both conformity and nonconformity – total conformity to what neuroscientists call your 'Deeper Self'… and total nonconformity when it comes to trying to be someone else – which is essentially attempting to be a bogus you, a phony you, a counterfeit you.

- Reinventing yourself is a form of vetting or repotting or recalibrating or retooling yourself. Make sure you're underwriting your new direction with the intention 'to your own Self be true.'

- Notice that nothing baffles those who have Ph.Ds in deceit, duplicity, fraud, hypocrisy, and pathological lying more than a person who has a high degree of Y☯Universally-based Authentegrity.

- Authentegrity is an integral part of friendship, companionship, partnership, kinship, and lifeship! Make sure those 'ships have come in' when it comes to defining your life.

- Be aware of any copycat choices you're making. If you find yourself moving into a copycat routine, ask yourself: "Why am I choosing imitation over Authentegrity?"

- You don't have to walk on water to exemplify a person who has Authentegrity. It's how you *walk your talk* that matters. So, walk the proverbial path on Y☯Universally-inspired feet.

- Constantly remind yourself that pound-for-pound, clear-cut choices based on integrity and fairness out-weigh prejudice and narrow-mindedness, no matter how much they throw their weight around.

- When people allow inaction, expediency, biases, politics, or disinterest to trump values, they're value-corrupted. So, say what you mean and mean what you say. To do otherwise means you have compromised the Authentegrity of your Y☯Universal Path.

Admit mistakes and take responsibility for your decisions and actions.

- Have absolutely no doubt that when you wed your values and beliefs with your choices, you show others it's possible to walk the road less traveled with dignity, grace, and Authentegrity.

- Honesty isn't the best policy, because honesty isn't a policy at all – it's a conviction which takes it far beyond the pale of mere policy. Honesty can't be mandated by edict or policy. Trust that honesty comes from incontestable conviction and unwavering Authentegrity.

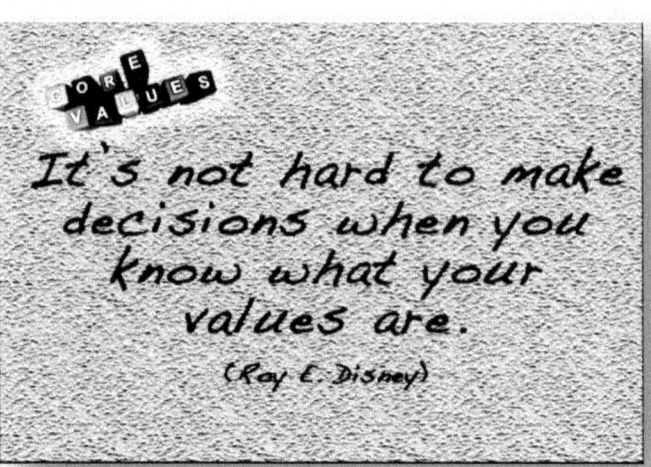

All I would tell people is to hold on to what was individual about themselves, not to allow their ambition for success to cause them to try to imitate the success of others. You've got to find it on your own terms.
(Harrison Ford)

Intuitive Wisdom

I ntuitive Wisdom is an inner knowing, uncommon sense. It expresses as an intuition that provides an immediate understanding of something, without the need for conscious reasoning or proof.

Let's look at an example. Have you ever done something that had a negative consequence, and immediately thought, "I knew I shouldn't have done that!" Or perhaps you had a feeling you should take some action, even though it made no practical sense – and the result was something powerful. **What you instinctively knew came from your Core Ability of "Intuitive Wisdom."** We all have that incredible ability within us, which we call on for inner guidance and discernment. When we focus on strengthening our Core Ability of Intuitive Wisdom, we are able to make decisions and take actions based on "uncommon sense." We trust that sixth sense of intuition and move forward regardless of what outer appearance may indicate. On a practical note, one could say that knowledge is the awareness that tomato is a fruit; Intuitive Wisdom is knowing NOT to use it in a fruit salad.

Our Intuitive Wisdom is the Core Ability to apply what we know (even if we are not aware we know it), and discern the right thing to do. We're talking about more than book learning ... Intuitive Wisdom is a deep inner knowing that goes beyond the facts.

The Color Yellow: Yellow is the color representing perception and understanding. It signifies the blend of experience and knowledge to create uncommon sense. Yellow is the color of Intuitive Wisdom. When you operate from that place of alignment, you are able to make wise choices, take appropriate risks, step into the unknown with confidence, and intuitively know what to do, as you are being true to the Extraordinary You!

Using the color YELLOW to strengthen your Core Ability of Intuitive Wisdom: If you want to strengthen your awareness of your Intuitive Wisdom, make yellow your color of focus. Choose to wear something yellow as part of your wardrobe; eat foods that are yellow in color (i.e., bananas, yellow squash, lemons); place items that are yellow in your environment (yellow flowers, a yellow stone, pictures with yellow being the dominant color).

While this may feel a little silly at first, allow yourself to give it a try without judgment. Become aware of how much more often you listen to your intuition; how much stronger your decisions become; how easily you know how to handle a situation, and how you are experiencing more Intuitive Wisdom in your life.

A Sampling of Hors d'Oeuvres Related to Intuitive Wisdom

- See Intuitive Wisdom as a cognitive firewall that protects you from irrational thinking, ridiculous choices, and preposterous actions.

- The still point, the Divine Singularity within, is where your Intuitive Wisdom lives. Visit it every chance you get. It'll keep you above the fray of indecisiveness and wrong turns.

- Recognize that Intuitive Wisdom is logic in a hurry.

- Tune into your Intuitive Wisdom so you can specialize in heart-to-head resuscitation.

- Purposefully sequester yourself into a few moments of quiet solitude and rest as an intuitive 'retreat forward' as you start each day. It's starting your busy day on the right foot. MetaSpiritually, your right foot symbolizes deep spiritual understanding and the left foot stands for spiritual knowledge.

- When you *intuit* something, you're really '*in-to-it*' – you know, at a deeper level of knowing that by-passes the slower rational mind's linear reasoning process. Enjoy '*in-to-iting*' as a regular cutting-edge spiritual practice.

- Recognize that emotion usually trumps reason and Intuitive Wisdom generally trumps the linear reasoning process.

- Isn't it fun to know that superior intuition leaves conventional rationality a trail of popcorn to follow?

- Note that the moment an intuitive thought surfaces and its insight is vocalized and/or converted into a corresponding behavior, you experience what we call parallel playfulness.

- Sometimes you just have to trust your gut more than your head.

- The drudgery of highly analytical thinking involves 99% perspiration. However, the lightning speed of intuition will save you from working up a sweat at all.

- The brain itself is dialed-up for intuitive flashes. Why? Because the synaptic connections that create intuitive highways in your neural networks are reconfigured gray matter that allows you to see things you didn't see before in a flash. So, dial-up your intuitive intelligence every chance you get.

Notice that the world of outer appearances bows to Intuitive Wisdom.

- Our superior Intuitive Wisdom is the 'Voice of the Silence.' It's the 'Voice of Nāda (Kung tone – Middle F).

- Realize that Intuitive Wisdom isn't a product of formal schooling, but of being schooled by your Extraordinary Divine Nature, which is the Cosmic Superintendent of your particular Y☯Universe.

- When you think about it, Intuitive Wisdom is a form of upward mobility. It simply means you've 'upped your consciousness' to a higher, more mobile, inner knowing. So, be upwardly mobile so you can experience the Y☯Universal Prosperity that will illuminate your spiritual path.

- See Intuitive Wisdom as an internal cognitive search engine that cuts through the malware of doubt, ambiguity, and fear.

- ☯ Notice that oftentimes the bandwidth of Intuitive Wisdom runs rings around an analytical mindset.

- ☯ Trust that the ability to let go of obsolete values, of non-productive lifestyle habits, and self-nullifying attitudes that sabotage your overall well-being is an essential part of how your Intuitive Wisdom fortifies you.

- ☯ Find a quiet place, free from interruptions and distractions. You'll be surprised what messages will come to you if you allow yourself a few cubic feet of silence. Listen to all of the whispers emanating from your Intuitive Wisdom, urging you toward Y☯Universal Prosperity.

- ☯ Wherever your heart leads you, it leads you to Truth. Trust it. Have compassion for those who have lost touch with its cadence, who cannot hear or refuse to listen to their heart's Intuitive Wisdom.

- ☯ Uncommon sense is the seventh sense, right after intuition (the sixth sense). It's an essential part of your make-up to keep the other six senses from making fools of themselves— and you from being guilty by association.

- ☯ Use at least six of the thirty "hearing aids" you came into skin school with – sight, touch, smell, hearing, taste, and intuition. (Did you know humans have at least 30 senses? According to a study by New Scientist, there are 33! Just Google "33 human senses" to read more about them.)

- ☯ Each choice you make *really* matters. Each choice *becomes* what is yours to do! So, choose wisely, practically, and intuitively, because there are absolutely no ordinary moments when it comes to expressing who you really are. And once you choose, do it with Authentegrity and Joy!

- Don't block your soul growth by allowing your material interests and over-consumptive sense appetites to trump your inner wisdom and powers of discernment.

- Trust that your Intuitive Wisdom will lead you into an inner expansiveness and spaciousness in consciousness. You'll experience profound awakenings that bring inner peace and clarity beyond egocentric understanding, which open the mysteries of life.

- Your Brow Chakra, called the Third Eye, is one of the most mystical areas of your psyche. It's the seat of wisdom and higher esoteric understanding, making it a highly intuitive and insightful center.

- Know that in Jewish mysticism, *chocmah*, or *chokhmah*, stands for wisdom, and links wisdom and divine intuition together.

- Realize that knowledge, no matter how correct or expertish (*We love making up those kind of words!*), will never replace wisdom and common sense.

- Put your common sense, better judgment, and patience in gear before you put your mouth in motion.

- Keep in mind that the trouble with preoccupied people who think too little is they get lost in thought when they try to think too much. The reason some people get lost in thought is because thinking itself is such unfamiliar territory.

- Don't hesitate to pass the Golden Baton to others who are on the path. A 'golden baton' is ancient wisdom being passed from spiritual teachers to students, who become spiritual teachers, who pass it on to their students, who pass it on, etc.

> Know well what leads you forward
> and what holds you back,
> and choose the path that leads to
> **WISDOM**
> (Buddha)

The most beautiful and profound emotion we can experience is the sensation of the mystical. It is the power of all true sciences. (The one) to whom this emotion is a stranger, who can no longer wonder and stand rapt in awe, is as good as dead. To know what is impenetrable to us really exists, manifesting itself as the highest wisdom and the most radiant beauty which our dull faculties can comprehend only in the most primitive form – this knowledge, this feeling is at the center of our true being. (Albert Einstein)

Inner Strength

When you develop **Inner Strength** as one of your Core Abilities, you will be able to meet any challenge, disappointment, or difficulty with a high degree of confidence and poise. This Core Ability is the epitome of grit, resilience, mental toughness, tenacity, determination, and fortitude – all of which you already possess at a deep level.

Having strong Inner Strength allows you to draw on your internal resources, your mental skills, and your physical capabilities to confront difficulties of all kinds. With this Core ability operating at its highest, most elevated level, you draw upon your energy and stamina so that when you face challenges that deplete you of energy and material resources, you still have enough willpower left within you to act confidently and decisively. You can stay the course, and do what you have chosen is yours to do. You can call on Inner Strength when you must move through a difficult task, work through a challenging life situation, or walk by a bowl of M&Ms!

The Color Russet Brown: Russet Brown is the color of stability, depth, and tenacity. It signifies strength and maturity. Russett Brown is the color of Inner Strength because it signifies your roots, which go deep within your being and allow you to accomplish things that may appear difficult, challenging, or even impossible, knowing you are claiming the Extraordinary You!

Using the color RUSSET BROWN to strengthen your Core Ability of Inner Strength: If you want to strengthen your awareness of your Inner Strength, make russet brown your color of focus. Choose to wear something brown as part of your wardrobe; eat foods that are brown in color (i.e., nuts, brown rice, beef, chocolate, coffee); place items that are brown in your environment (wooden sculptures, pine cone arrangement, a brown stone, pictures with brown being the dominant color).

While this may feel a little silly at first, allow yourself to give it a try without judgment. Become aware of how much more tenacious and resilient you are; how much stronger your actions become; how easily you are able to see projects through to the end, and how you are experiencing more Inner Strength in your life.

A Sampling of Hors d'Oeuvres Related to Inner Strength

- ☯ Recognize that there's an *empower-tarian* dimension at the center of your nature. Neuroscientists call it your 'Deeper Self.' We call it your Soul Signature, the Extraordinary You. It's the tenacious you, the confident you, the poised you, the brilliant you, the resilient you, the Y☯Universal You.

- ☯ Be aware that mental toughness requires a lot of eye, hand, foot, ear, and thick skin coordination.

- ☯ Reflecting on the past so you can learn from it, but not dwell on it, is a telltale sign of the tremendous Inner Strength that comes from your Y☯Universe.

- ☯ Inner strength is not genetic, and it certainly is a lot more than phonetic. It's an inner resolve that's simply kinetic. It means replacing doubts, fear, and nagging lack of confidence with an indomitable will.

- ☯ See any alphabet of troubles as a symphony of your unfoldment.

- ☯ Remind yourself that Inner Strength gives you the chutzpah to lean into adversity instead of back-stepping, or back-sliding, to try to keep your balance.

- ☯ Know that 'kindling your Inner Strength and resolve within' means having more willpower than won't power.

- ☯ Do not hesitate to affirm that using Inner Strength to respond to the bad things that happen to you on your spiritual journey generally keeps you on the path to experience the best things that will happen to you.

- ☯ Realize that the rough edges of outer circumstances require smooth resolve of your Y☯Universal Strength.

- ☯ Keep in mind that Inner Strength is a powerful emotional firewall that can't be penetrated by fear, hardship, adversity, naysayers, or doubt.

- ☯ Recognize that Inner Strength isn't a bunch of amino acids and protein codes bumping into each other. It's what causes those amino acids and protein codes to jump into action.

- ☯ See Inner Strength as replacing a wishbone with a backbone.

- ☯ Be aware that mental toughness is the ability to absorb the unexpected, stay positive, and remain supple and non-defensive in the face of an increasingly pressure-filled and complex skin school experience.

Trust that Inner Strength means making seemingly insurmountable mountains into incredible mountaintop experiences.

- ☯ Know that fortitude and composure increase your recovery rate (your bounce back rate) no matter what setbacks you encounter on your way toward mastering your skin school experience.

- ☯ Be cognizant of the fact that physical strength is measured by what we can lift, push, or pull. Inner strength is measured by what we can bear.

- ☯ Affirm that Inner Strength means not allowing speed bumps, detours, or wrong turns to determine the end of the journey.

- People who have a high degree of Inner Strength know that the proverbial expression that asks whether the glass is half empty or half full is missing the point: the glass is refillable! That's a Y☯Universal Truth!

- Note that mature Inner Strength sees doubts, ambiguity, fear, puzzlement, and confusion as false evidences appearing real.

- Know that reinventing yourself takes constant focus, unmitigated commitment, patience, a healthy sense of humor, and Inner Strength.

- Tested by the crucible of experience, you either succeed or fail, move forward or are incapacitated, find meaning and purpose or become lost and bitter. Exposed to the harsh realities of life, many people choose to cocoon themselves rather than depend on their Inner Strength. By recognizing that, make it a practice to turn millstones into milestones.

When the Truth squares off at you today, welcome it with an open heart and a receptive mind, Inner Strength, and a healthy pragmatism.

- Decide whether the moral limits you set today spring from conscience or convenience, inner turmoil or Inner Strength.

- Become less of a walking pharmacy by eating right, thinking positively, meditating daily, exercising more, and depending more on your Inner Strength.

- Have the Inner Strength to resolve a long-standing family issue. Heal a hurt. Right a wrong. Mend what's broken.

- Stop *shoulding* on yourself and others. Replace worthless *shoulds* and *ought to's* with the resolve to do better, be better, think better, hear better, feel better, speak better, and act better the next time.

- Stop worrying about the squalls and save your energy, Inner Strength, and creativity for the emotional hurricanes and tsunamis in life.

- In work as in life, you must be willing to do the right thing. And the *right thing* is to be courageous enough to have the Inner Strength it takes to align your human self with your Divine Nature. When you accomplish that, your Y☯Universe is the right place to be.

- Never yield to the growl of a dog, the tears of a crocodile, the cravings of a vulture, or the howling of a hyena.

- Constantly remind yourself that with plenty of intelligence, conscience, faith, and courage to guide you, you can help bring the human race from a rudderless mass of self-interest to the common ground of mutual respect, loving kindness, compassion, dignity, tolerance, and goodwill.

Most people achieved their greatest successes one step beyond what looked like their greatest failure. (Brian Tracy)

Optimistic Spirit

An Optimistic Spirit allows you to maintain a positive outlook regardless of the appearances. With an Optimistic Spirit, you are able to move beyond any and all failures, disappointments, difficult situations, or negative experiences, because you hold a world view that recognizes the innate good that exists within every opportunity. It is not the same as seeing the world through rose-colored glasses! Being optimistic is an attitude that sees situations and events as being temporary and controllable, although the situation itself may not be fully understood. Optimism is characterized by an attitude of hope for future conditions unfolding in a beneficial way, as well as seeing the potential in situations and people even when it is not obvious. A broader view of optimism, well stated by Einstein, is the understanding that "our lives—past, present and future—operate by laws of optimization and that the universe is wired in our behalf." Living from an Optimistic Spirit may not change the situations you face, but it can absolutely put things into a healthier, more life-affirming perspective that opens your mind to solutions, and puts you in a position to positively influence the behavior of others for enhanced results.

The Color Orange: Orange is the color of warmth, happiness, and optimism. It is a color which keeps us motivated and focused on the positive aspects of life. Orange is the color of an Optimistic Spirit because, when you operate from a belief in the positive side of life, you can overcome all forms of negativity and disappointment, knowing you are being true to the Extraordinary You … the Truth of who you really are!

Using the color ORANGE to strengthen your Core Ability of Optimistic Spirit: If you want to strengthen your awareness of your Optimistic Spirit, make Orange your color of focus. Choose to wear something orange as part of your wardrobe; eat foods that are orange in color (oranges, sweet potatoes, carrots, cheddar cheese, Doritos, pumpkin, cantaloupe, peaches etc.); place items that are orange in your environment (orange flowers, an orange stone, pictures with orange as a dominant color). You may even want to use orange ink or markers when you write.

While this may feel a little silly at first, allow yourself to give it a try without judgment. Become aware of how much more positive you feel, how you are focusing in ways to use everything for good, and how you are experiencing the Optimistic Spirit in your life.

A Sampling of Hors d'Oeuvres Related to Optimistic Spirit

- Define the lifestyle you want; then wrap your work around it.

- Anesthetize every error thought, self-denigrating inclination, and each self-defeating obstacle that surfaces in your conscious awareness.

- Be philanthropic! As a matter of fact, be sooooo philanthropic that philanthropy will be associated with you personally: there's Cher-lanthropy, Bil-lanthropy, Judy-lanthropy, Jim-lanthropy, (insert your first name)-lanthropy, etc.

> *Recognize that opportunities knock more than once, because that's the nature of opportunities.*

- Prime yourself for serendipitous experiences so you can leap over RUTs (rigid unyielding thinking).

- Don't hesitate to kick a negativity bias to the curb every chance you get.

- One of the chief rationales of optimists just might be: Give me a cup of coffee to change the things I can and a piece of dark chocolate to accept the things I can't change right now.

- Optimism doesn't wait on all of the facts. It also listens to the can-guru inside of you.

- Optimists realize that disappointments and even failures are places of reference, not places of residence.

- Being positively positive, what we call super-charged optimism, is an optimist's default strategy. However, people with a positive mindset are neither naïve, nor blind to the facts, or even in denial of grim realities. They simply believe in optimizing all available options.

- The *prism* of positivity sees the *prison* of negativity as only a speed bump, not a wall. Optimistic people know this. That's why they brush off negativity like lint off their clothing. So, practice 'lint' removal every chance you get.

- Optimism isn't fantasy at all. It affirms the underlying good in your Y☯Universe that underwrites everything.

- Science shows that those with an optimistic outlook tend to be more proactive when it comes to their health, have better cardiovascular health, a stronger immune system, generally earn a higher income, and tend to have more successful relationships.

- Looking for silver linings is where the line ends for negativity. That's what optimism is all about. Silver line all of your thinking, being and doing.

- Reflect on your 'Abandonment Rate.' In online marketing lingo, the abandonment rate refers to an online shopper leaving items in their virtual shopping cart but never completing the sale. From a MetaSpiritul perspective, the 'abandonment rate' is the rate at which we drop optimistic thoughts for negatively-charged thoughts, whims, and desires, and never go back to pick up our positivity.

- The 'acoustics of amnesty' are positive thoughts and feelings of relief, joy, and bliss we 'hear' when our errors are pardoned by our wise choices.

> What we want is not blind optimism, but flexible optimism!
>
> We must be able to use pessimism's keen sense of reality when we need it, but without having to dwell in its dark shadows.
>
>
> Martin Seligman

I simply used the energy it took to pout, and wrote the blues. (Duke Ellington)

Questioning Unquestioned Answers

Questioning Unquestioned Answers, (also known as thinking outside-the-box) is a Core Ability that encourages you to step outside the norm, challenge the status quo, think unconventionally, and view everything from a new, expanded perspective. It encourages you to question everything you believe to be a fact or a required way of doing things. What we're actually recommending is for you to change a period to a question mark as you problem-solve and innovate. For example, suppose someone says "Everyone has free will." It's time to change the period to a question mark: "Everyone has free will?" Perhaps the original statement is true, but perhaps it is merely echoing a dogmatic belief from your past that is ready to be re-examined, questioned, and updated. When we questioned that particular statement, for example, we changed our entire way of thinking about free will, and now say we all have "influenced will." (We considered explaining more about this, but our questioning nature said no!)

Using the Core Ability of Questioning Unquestioned Answers will prompt you to challenge any confirmation bias. Confirmation bias is a term used by psychologists to describe our tendency to only accept information that confirms a viewpoint we have already set in our minds, and reject any information that casts doubt on it. Thus, we become prisoners of our own assumptions and beliefs.

The Color Blue: Blue is the color representing self-expression and creativity. It signifies an ability to think beyond the predictable and known, and stretch into innovative solutions to situations. Blue is the color of Questioning Unquestioned Answers because when you operate from that place of alignment, you open your awareness to innovative ideas. You live in the awareness that you can always discover better ways to handle situations, come up with innovative solutions, and identify unique approaches to everything, as you remain true to the Extraordinary You!

Using the Color Blue: If you want to strengthen your awareness of your innate Questioning Unquestioned Answers Core Ability, make blue your color of focus. Choose to wear something blue as part of your wardrobe; eat foods that are blue in color (you are allowed to be creative, especially with this Core Ability! Consider blueberries, blue M&Ms, blue corn chips, Blue Diamond almonds — and don't forget bleu cheese!); place items that are blue in your environment (blue flowers, a blue stone, pictures with blue as a dominant color). You can even use blue ink or markers when you write.

While this may feel a little silly at first, allow yourself to give it a try without judgment. Become aware of how ideas seem to flow to you effortlessly, how much easier it feels to solve problems that crop up, and how you are experiencing a willingness – even an inner urge – to question the unquestioned answers in your life.

A Sampling of Hors d'Oeuvres Related to Questioning Unquestioned Answers

- Remember that your spiritual growth and human happiness aren't so much limited by unanswered questions as they are by mindlessly believing in unquestioned answers.

- Mutually agreeing to question unquestioned answers and then be open to the truths uncovered can postpone the end of human history. If we can do that internationally, nationally, regionally, locally, and individually, imagine what progress we could make!

- Not questioning unquestioned answers becomes a catch basin for dysfunctional dogmatic tribalism.

See order within chaos, rightness in absurdity, truth within ambiguity, opportunity in the midst of limitations, and the extraordinary in the ordinary.

- Scrub off unquestioned answers every chance you get by recognizing that the light of conventional lampposts keep many people comfortable with the status quo in the dark. Wipe any and all darkness from your Y☯Universe.

- Know when to say when, why to say when, what to say when, and where to say when.

- Get really good at replacing periods at the end of sentences with question marks. For example:

- Opportunity only knocks once. Opportunity only knocks once?
- Prayer is talking to God and meditation is listening to God. Prayer is talking to God and meditation is listening to God?

☯ Refuse to be imprisoned by unquestioned answers – which is living with the beliefs and opinions of other people's thinking and biases.

☯ Know that it's better to question an answer without settling it than to settle on an answer without questioning it. That's a Y☯Universal Truth.

☯ Losing most of our body heat through our head is an unquestioned answer that's been questioned scientifically, and proven to be untrue. There's nothing special about where we lose heat. In reality, we lose heat through any uncovered body surface. What other old beliefs are you still living with, as if they are truth?

☯ Understand that it isn't easy for a new idea to squeeze itself into a head that's much too comfortable with mindlessly believing in unquestioned answers.

☯ Realize that questions generally contain half the answer and answers usually demand another well-packaged question. Also, recognize that short questions generally have long answers and long questions tend to have short answers.

☯ Living in the questions keeps answers from flat-lining. So, live in a healthy Y☯Universe. Question all unquestioned answers.

- ☯ You can tell how knowledgeable people are by their answers, but you can see how wise and discerning they are by their questions. Makes sense, doesn't it?

- ☯ Questioning unquestioned answers forces tradition to curtsy to enlightened thought.

Recognize that thinking outside the proverbial box is swimming in your own stream of consciousness.

- ☯ Challenging traditional answers can give you an entirely different perspective. For instance, at a ballet, the women dance on their tiptoes. One of the questions that begs to be asked is – why don't they just hire taller dancers?

- ☯ Note that not questioning unquestioned answers could be considered complacency peddling.

- ☯ Not questioning unquestioned answers is where you may have stood yesterday. Realize that questioning unquestioned answers may very well indicate what you won't stand for today.

- ☯ Unlike most spiritual and scientific sojourns, where you have a premeditated and predetermined theoretical destination, the journey in MetaSpirituality is one of constant evolution, transformation, and questioning unquestioned answers.

- ☯ Adopt the view that questioning unquestioned answers is a corrective lens that helps expose the fictions retailed by mindless dogmas.

- *De veritate disputandum est (About matters of truth, dispute is fruitful).* What is and what isn't can be resolved by looking at proof vs. preference. Trust that the movement from what is disputed to what is no longer disputable can be gained by questioning unquestioned answers.

- Have little doubt that sometimes what many people call facts are only unquestioned answers, personal opinions, unfounded assumptions, and adopted biases that are generated to reduce uncertainty, confusion, and fear.

- "Why don't you read by the bright lamp instead of the flickering candle flame?" they questioned. The Sufi master smiled and explained, "The bright lamp over there attracts all the moths (unquestioned answers and assumptions), leaving me free to read in peace here."

- The truth or fiction lies dormant in every unquestioned answer. Which one do you want to prevail?

- *You should change your toothbrush after a cold* is an unquestioned answer that's been questioned and proven false. After recovering from a cold, your body has built up immunity to those germs, making it virtually impossible to be infected again by the same virus. Continue to clean your toothbrush, of course, because that's just plain good hygiene.

- Remind yourself that there's always plenty of "asking" room when you're questioning unquestioned answers.

- Questioning unquestioned answers is the wise practice of demanding the credentials of supposed facts. Legitimate facts have staying power. And they have staying power because they are, well, proven to be true.

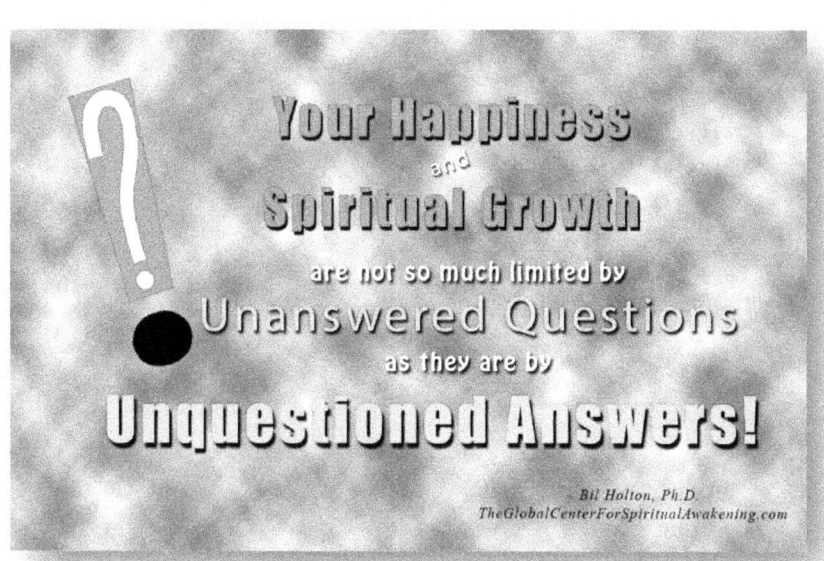

No one is dumb who is curious. The people who don't ask questions remain clueless throughout their lives. (Neil deGrasse Tyson)

Self-Reliance

Self-reliance is based on what psychologists call an 'internal locus of control,' which means that many of the events in one's life, whether positive or negative, are mediated by how we respond to them. This includes our beliefs, attitudes, values, preparation, effort, and results. We agree with that and believe it's a great psychological concept. However, we've come up with our own 'internal control' concept ourselves, based on our MetaSpiritual perspective. And we've named it an 'internal *lotus* of control,' which adds a spiritual dimension to an otherwise benign psychological mental health concept. Consider how '*lotus*' instead of 'locus' amps up the spiritual aspects of the concept.

Recognizing and using our Core Ability of Self-Reliance, or Internal Lotus of Control, takes us out of the victim consciousness, and moves us into the active role of taking charge of our lives. We learn from our mistakes, take actions to manifest our desires, and choose to claim whatever level of control is ours in any situation. Studies performed by the Mayo Clinic link Self-Reliance with improved physical health, mental health, and quality of life in people with diverse conditions such as migraines, diabetes, kidney disease, HIV, and epilepsy.

The Color Purple: Purple is the color of depth of understanding and transformation. It represents Self-Reliance because it signifies your ability to transform any life situation or circumstance through your power of choice. It represents your ability to claim responsibility for your results, knowing you are making decisions, interpreting information, and living as the Extraordinary You!

Using the Color Purple: If you want to strengthen your awareness of your Self-Reliance, make purple your color of focus. Choose to wear something purple as part of your wardrobe; eat foods that are purple in color (grapes, egg plant. purple cabbage, beets, plums, etc.); place items that are purple in your environment (purple flowers, a purple stone, pictures with purple as a dominant color). Use purple ink or markers when you write.

While this may feel a little silly at first, allow yourself to give it a try without judgment. Become aware of how much more in control you feel, how your choices are more powerful and self-affirming, and how you are experiencing Self-Reliance in your life.

A Sampling of Hors d'Oeuvres Related to Self-Reliance

- ☯ Keep in mind that sometimes self-reliance means you've 'got your own back.'

- ☯ Approach life with the cumulative force of your personality, experience, authentegrity, intuition, genuineness, and Divine Nature, because it'll fortify your self-reliance – which is a key personal quality in creating Y☯Universal Prosperity.

- ☯ See self-discipline, self-mastery, and self-control as the trinity of self-reliance.

- ☯ Know that one of the best places to find a willing and helping hand is at the end of your own arm.

- ☯ Self-reliance doesn't mean isolating yourself from others. It means believing in your own talents and abilities to the extent that they will guarantee your self-determination, personal autonomy, and self-sufficiency.

> *Make it okay to be a 'take charge-aholic,' and not a 'cop-out-aholic.'*

- ☯ Self-reliant people increase their 'bounce rate.' They know that there's nothing they can't bounce back from. If there's anything you need to bounce back from, take a slow deep breath and exhale slowly through your mouth, be Zenful, and then increase your 'bounce rate.'

- ☯ Realize that self-reliant people make it a point to 'know' themselves before they 'no' themselves.

- Self-reliance has a lot of other positive 'self-strength' company: self-control, self-discipline, self-motivation, self-actualization, self-awareness, self-confidence, self-starter, self-accountability, self-responsibility, self-knowledge, self-mastery, self-acknowledgment, etc. Cultivate all of these 'self-strengths.' They'll help you create Y☯Universal Prosperity.

- Understand that there's an inverse relationship between reliance on the world of outer appearances and the reliance on your own instincts, knowledge and experience.

- Always remember, being self-reliant means you're non-conforming, unsubmissive, unlabel-able, and definitely not prone to saying 'uncle.'

- Self-reliance is an inner might that serves as a sort of Kevlar vest, protecting you from the slings and arrows of skin school.

- Remind yourself that self-reliance is one of your best accessories. Never leave home without it.

- Did you know that people who have a high degree of self-reliance have 'unstoppable' as their middle name?

- Notice that people who have a high degree of self-reliance live by superior discernment, not by happenstance; are motivated, not manipulated; turn can't into can; and keep promises, not make excuses.

- Coffee in one hand and confidence in the other seems to be all the preparation a self-reliant person needs.

- Self-reliance doesn't mean over-reliance. And it doesn't mean stretching yourself too thin. And it certainly doesn't mean wearing yourself out. The foundation for self-reliance is based on past performance as a marker for success. It's built on reality, not fantasy.

- Trust that self-reliant people would rather live on the cutting edge instead of a dull edge.
- Self-Reliance means knowing who to ask for help, how to build a strong network, and when you need to reach out to others.
- You're the most influential, reliable, notable, and important person you'll ever talk to, communicate with, take advice from, and be with. So, optimize self-reliance as one of the core qualities of Y☯Universal Prosperity.

Having a strong sense of controlling one's life is a more dependable predictor of positive feelings of well-being than any of the objective conditions of life we have considered.
(Angus Campbell, researcher)

Giving Consciousness

A Giving Consciousness is critical for connecting with the Extraordinary You. Why? Because living from a Giving Consciousness implies that you have a consciousness of abundance instead of a consciousness of lack.

By strengthening our giving consciousness, we're in a position to create an atmosphere of generosity, which allows us to serve others better, because this 'sharing spirit' literally ignites a philanthropic spirit in us and in others. Added benefits come to us in the form of increased happiness, satisfaction, and inner peace. We're not making this up! There's research to confirm it.

A Giving Consciousness operates from the mindset of giving without any expectation or attachment to outcomes. It seems to be an Rx for the whole body. And it's also the royal road, the noble path to connecting with what neuroscientists call your Deeper Self, and what we refer to as the Extraordinary You.

The Color Green: Green is the color representing growth and generosity. It signifies an awareness of the unending cycle of giving and receiving. Green is the color of a Giving Consciousness because when you operate from that place of alignment, you are always on the lookout of ways to give freely, knowing that as you live from this awareness, you always receive more than you give.

Using the Color Green: If you want to strengthen your awareness of your Giving Consciousness, make green your color of focus. Choose to wear something green as part of your wardrobe; eat foods that are green in color (i.e., string beans, collards, peas, kale, spinach, broccoli, lima beans, kiwi, pistachio ice cream, etc.); place green in your environment (green plants, a green stone, a picture with green as the dominant color); use green ink or markers when you write.

While this may feel a little silly at first, allow yourself to give it a try without being judgmental. Become aware of how your Giving Consciousness is strengthened, how you notice more opportunities for spontaneous generosity, and how you experience living in a Giving Consciousness mindset.

A Sampling of Hors d'Oeuvres Related to Giving Consciousness

- Give to give; don't give to get. Giving to get isn't giving. When you think about it, it's a form of entitlement – you know, *quid pro quo*.

- Be cognizant of the fact that people who are generous enjoy higher levels of positive emotions; are more alert, alive and awake; are more joyful, express more optimism and happiness; are more helpful, generous and compassionate; are more forgiving and more outgoing; and tend to feel less lonely and isolated.

- A few of the YOUniversal benefits people with a giving consciousness receive is the knowledge that they're doing their part to improve the world, that they're raising the spiritual octave of human consciousness, and affirming that giving is one of the higher human callings.

> *Don't measure generosity by the size of your gift, but by the size of your giving consciousness.*

- Take the initiative when it comes to giving, so you can lift the self-esteem of others instead of making someone feel inferior or unworthy.

- Generate an atmosphere of hospitality and caring by radiating a warm and inviting spirit.

- Realize that you can't offer your generosity too soon, because you never know how soon it could be too late for someone needing, but not receiving, a generous act.

- Realize that it's hard to have a true giving consciousness if you're grasping tightly on to your self-righteousness, your dogmatic belief system, your professed superiority, your false assumptions about others, and your definition of who's worthy of your help.

- Give 'till it Hertz, that is, give at 639 Hz (the Heart Chakra Hz in the Solfeggio frequency).

- Know that non-monetary gifts, such as time, encouragement, faith-lifts, hope, laughter, smiles, hospitality, service, and forgiveness all have considerable life-changing value.

- Generous givers are answerers to the cries of the less fortunate, cheerleaders to those who feel unworthy, and preservers of human dignity and self-worth for those who've been marginalized.

- When it comes to giving generously, some people stop at nothing. Their holding back is based on a lack consciousness which keeps them poverty-bound.

- Upping your giving is downing your lack consciousness.

- The gravity of having a habit of not being generous or philanthropic is depravity of one's soul.

- Understand the Zen concept of non-attachments. By that we mean giving serves as a way to eliminate one's selfishness and desire for unnecessary attachments.

- Rejoice in a penchant for giving; to constantly cultivate goodwill; to help make other people happier; to bring more warmth, joy and generosity to the world.

- Value the intangibles flowing toward you from others – things like: goodwill, fondness, respect, appreciation, and love. Move past the reluctance to accept what's offered, to always appreciate someone else's generosity, and enjoy the pleasures of receiving.
- When it comes to material things, know when enough is enough, so you cultivate a consciousness of enough. Why? Because you are rich in direct proportion to what material things you can do without.
- You can't out-give what's in the Field of Infinite Potential.

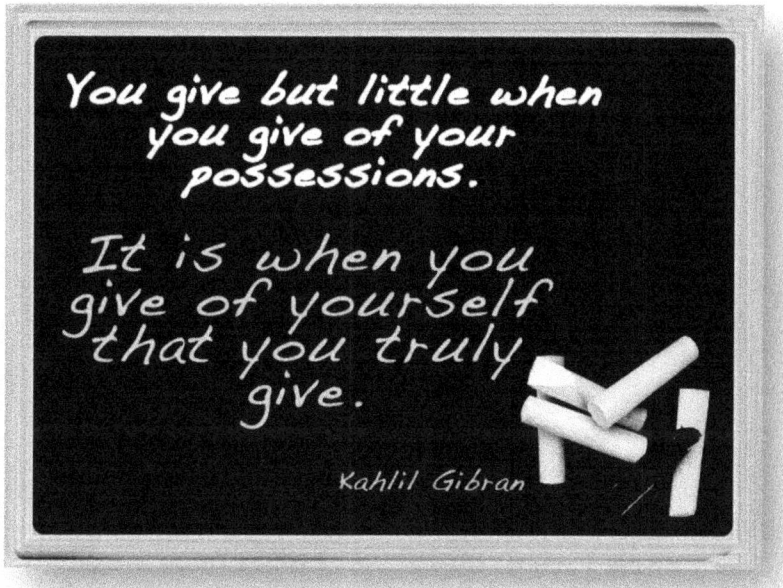

You give but little when you give of your possessions.

It is when you give of yourself that you truly give.

Kahlil Gibran

Too often we underestimate the power of a touch, a smile, a kind word, a listening ear, an honest compliment, or the smallest act of caring, all of which have the potential to turn a life around.

(Leo Buscaglia)

The Four Foundational Activities to Include in Your Spiritual Practice

We recommend the following four Foundational Spiritual Activities to strengthen and grow your ability to use all of your Seven Core Abilities, and experience the highest levels of Health, Happiness, Inner Peace, and Financial Security … as you achieve YOUniversal Prosperity!

Each of these Keystone Activities can be accomplished through innumerable styles, types, and activities. We encourage you to try as many different types as possible, to help you broaden the scope and depth of your Spiritual Practice. The goal is to include some form of each of these four Foundational Activities in your life every day!

The Four Foundational Spiritual Activities

- Meditation
- Release
- Forgiveness
- Gratitude

You can find lots of tips and strategies related to these four Foundational Activities on our website:

https://unitycenterforyouniversalprosperity.com/blog-2/

Use these four Foundational Activities to make your life a spiritual practice, and master the art of living as you walk the spiritual path on practical, positive, prosperous feet!

About Bil & Cher Holton

Combine a flair for the dramatic, a deep understanding of MetaSpiritual teachings, an ability to think outside the box, a penchant for questioning unquestioned answers, and a knack for bringing scientific research and spiritual practices to life in practical ways, and you have defined the dynamic duo who are at the heart of their nonprofit Unity Center For Y☯Universal Prosperity.

In 2005, the Holtons made the decision to follow their hearts, and entered into a spiritual training program that led them to become ordained Unity ministers. After eight years serving in the pulpit ministry, they're now committed to their global spiritual ministries. They've published over 70 books, have amped-up their New Thought perspectives into what they call Enlightened Thought perspectives, and have presented workshops and spiritual cafes all over the country. Their spiritual mission is to lead, guide, and inspire people all over the world to awaken to their Divine Nature so they can live faithfully, lovingly, and wisely at the speed of their Enlightenment.

On a personal note, the Holtons like to push the envelope and maintain their zest for life by taking what they call "Indiana Jones Adventures," such as white-water rafting, sky diving, fire walking, and deep-dive sitting meditational experiences. American-style ballroom dancing is also in their DNA. Although they've retired their competitive dance shoes, they continue to dance in the modest ballroom they've built upstairs in their home. They live in North Carolina, and love spending time with their two sons, beautiful daughters-in-law, seven grandchildren, and one great-grandson.

An Invitation From Bil and Cher

We invite you to visit our website to take advantage of all the free resources we provide, and check out our Events schedule. You'll find us at:

UnityCenterForYOUniversalProsperity.com/
(or ucfyp.com for short)

If you'd like a weekly inspiration, please sign up for our Monday Musings:
https://unitycenterforyouniversalprosperity.com/monday-musings/

And be sure to check out our products and services, all conveniently in one place at HoltonProductMall.com/

We also invite you to take a peek at our Spiritual Awakening and Sacred Path Mentoring Packages, where you can work with us through a systematic process of spiritual growth, join in with lots of deep-dive Zoom sessions and retreats, and be part of our online global community of people who consider themselves more spiritual than religious.

Please contact us to learn more about our services, and explore ways we can work with you or your groups. We offer virtual and live services, and would welcome the opportunity of talking with you! Our email address is: UCFYPministers@gmail.com/

Our heartfelt vision is to create an uplifting spiritual community where people feel loved, safe, and respected so they can master the art of living in skin school as they walk the spiritual path on practical, positive, and prosperous feet.

We love what we do, and we'd love you to be a part of it!
Namaste!

A Sampling of Other Books by Revs. Drs. Bil & Cher Holton

Revs. Drs. Bil and Cher Co-authored:
- *Life-Changing Spiritual Practices, Volumes 1-12*
- *Spiritually Speaking: A Metaphysical Interpretation of Spiritual, Religious, and Modern Day Secular Terms*
- *Power Up Your Life: Accessing Your Twelve Powers to Achieve Health, Happiness, Abundance, and Inner Peace*
- *Reconciling the Church's Science Phobia: The Dance Between Science and Spirituality*
- *Straight Talk About Spiritual Stuff*
- *Right Thoughts, Right Choices, Right Actions: 200 of the Best Choices Unity People Will Ever Make*
- *Business Prayers for Millennium Managers*
- *The Manager's Short Course to a Long Career*
- *Crackerjack Choices: 200 of the Best Choices You Will Ever Make*
- *Suppose: Questions to Turbo-Charge Your Business and Your Life*
- *From Ballroom to Bottom Line ... In Business and Life*
- *Seriously: 25 Cringe-Worthy Phrases Leaders Use That Rob Them of Their Credibility ... and How to Retool Them!*

Revs. Drs. Bil & Cher Co-Editors, contributors, & publisher of the following anthologies:
- *Life, Work, and Money From a Woman's Perspective* (Foreword by Kay Yow)
- *Rekindling the Human Spirit* (Foreword Interview with Jamie Valvano Howard)
- *That's My Story and I'm Sticking to It!* (Foreword by John Goddard)

Rev. Dr. Bil authored:
- *Gospel of Matthew: New Metaphysical Version*

Gospel of Mark; New Metaphysical Version
Gospel of Luke; New Metaphysical Version
Gospel of John; New Metaphysical Version
The Book of Revelation, New Metaphysical Version
Rev. Bil Unplugged and Unedited
Ruff-Housing with Religious Dogma
Matthew Revisited
Mark Revisited
Luke Revisited
John Revisited
Meta New Testament, Vol. 1
Meta New Testament, Vol. 2
The Lazarus Legacy
America Is My Home
Twist of Fate (novel)
Ultimate Betrayal (novel)
Silent Echoes (novel)
Déjá Vu All Over Again (novel, sequel to Silent Echoes)

Rev Dr. Cher Holton authored:

Extraordinary Leadership: Connecting With Your Seven Core Abilities to Bring Out the Extraordinary Abilities in Others
Living at the Speed of Life: Staying in Control in a World Gone Bonkers!
Power Up Card Decks

Books coauthored with Rev. Dr. Paul Hasselbeck:

Applying Heart-Centered Metaphysics
PowerUP: The Twelve Powers Revisited as Accelerated Abilities
Get Over It: The Truth About What You Know That Just Ain't So!
Get Over These Too: More Truth About What You Know That Just Ain't So!

Credits:

Cover Design and book layout: Cher Holton

Image Credits (all used with permission):

Pg. 4: pixabay.com, 11050_1920
Pg. 7: Cher Holton
Pg. 23: Cher Holton
Pg. 27: Cher Holton and graphicstock.com
Pg. 30: Wikimedia Commons
Pg. 31: Cher Holton, clipart.com
Pg. 36: dreamstime.com, 117232220
Pg. 40: Cher Holton and storyblocks.com, MymSJQDu
Pg. 43: Cher Holton
Pg. 45: Cher Holton and clipart.com
Pg. 51: dreamstime.com, I_40426775
Pg. 53: dreamstime.com, I_129077002
Pg. 56: clipart.com, 1.21533033
Pg. 57: pixabay.com, 2839706_1280
Pg. 64: pixabay.com-1920894_1280
Pg. 66: Cher Holton and graphicstock.com
Pg. 68: Pixabay.com, 41753_1280
Pg. 77: Cher Holton (Highland Lake Resort)
Pg. 81: Cher Holton and dreamstime.com, I_35103425
Pg. 91: dreamstime.com, I_70702037
Pg. 92: clipart.com, 7530988
Pg. 94: clipart.com, 109995754
Pg. 96: dreamstime.com, 23621319
      Cher Holton and clipart.com, 24649810
Pg. 101: pixabay.com, 5799526_1920
Pg. 117: pixabay.com, 4761224_1920
Pg. 120: creative commons
Pg. 121: unsplash.com, 1474557157379-8aa74a6ef541
Pg. 122: creative commons, Pinterest
Pg. 124: dreamstime.com, I_157969215
Pg. 125: creative commons
Pg. 126: graphicstock.com
      dreamstime.com, I_100417337
Pg. 131: dreamstime.com, 58228213
Pg. 134: pixabay.com, 2048252_1920
Pg. 144: pixabay.com, 104031_1920
Pg. 146: dreamstime.com, I_26427282
Pg. 148: pixabay.com, 1197351_1920

Pg. 153: Cher Holton

Pg. 154: graphicstock.com, 866110617_14d583e540

Pg. 155: Cher Holton and clipart.com, 19396486

Pg. 157: dreamstime.com, I_50287140

Pg. 158: graphicstock.com, M1|102w

Pg. 159: pixabay.com, 396265_1920
   Cher Holton and clipart.com

Pg. 160: iStock.com, 000022382935

Pg. 161: clipart.com, 109513746

Pg. 166: pixabay.com, 148815

Pg. 168: pixabay.com, 1167618_1920

Pg. 169: dreamstime.com, 8683396

Pg. 174: pixabay.com, 5018088_1920

Pg. 181: dreamstime.com, 32980117

Pg. 183: dreamstime.com, 23985735

Pg. 192: dreamstime.com, I_26652450

Pg. 195: Cher Holton and clipart.com

Pg. 201: dreamstime.com, 31808485

Pg. 205: dreamstime.com, I_48356438

Pg. 215: dreamstime.com, 30682516

Pg. 220: graphicstock.com, GkD7n-i

Pg. 223: Cher Holton

Pg. 227: Cher Holton and storyblocks.com

Pg. 232: Cher Holton

Pg. 233: shutterstock.com

Pg. 239: Cher Holton

Pg. 241: sxc.com, 1391023_83715493

Pg. 247: Cher Holton and clipart.com

Pg. 249: Cher Holton

Pg. 253: Cher Holton

Pg. 255: Cher Holton; clipart.com 60508525 and dreamstime.com, 21668821

Pg. 261: Cher Holton

Pg. 263: Cher Holton and iStock.com. 000004802614

Pg. 267: Cher Holton and graphicstock.com

Pg. 269: Cher Holton and dreamstime.com, 1082838

Pg. 273: Cher Holton and clipart.com

Pg. 277: Gaillyn.photography@gmail.com

www.ingramcontent.com/pod-product-compliance
Lightning Source LLC
Chambersburg PA
CBHW070807170426
43200CB00007B/850